THE
WAY WE LIVE
NOW

General Editor: Gerald Konyn

Illustrations by Judy Deykin

The
Way We Live
Now

Bernard Levin

LARGE PRINT
MASTERWORKS

First published in Great Britain
in 1984 by Jonathan Cape Ltd
30 Bedford Square, London, WC1B 3EL

© Bernard Levin 1984
Published in Large Print 1989
by arrangement with Jonathan Cape Ltd
A joint imprint of ISIS Large Print Books,
55 St. Thomas' Street, Oxford OX1 1JG
and Guild Large Print Books Ltd
25 High Street, Lewes, Sussex

Photosetting in Times 18 pt by
Futura Typesetters, Hove, Sussex
printed in Great Britain by
Antony Rowe Ltd, Chippenham, Witlshire

ISBN 1 85290 019 9

Jacket design by Douglas Quiggan
and Robert Soudain. Title page
design by Robert Soudain. Portrait of
Bernard Levin by Bob Bowdige

CONTENTS

The valley of dry bones

There was a strange and little-remarked story the other day which has been echoing in my head; not surprisingly, as it was composed almost entirely of echoes. It concerned bones, human bones, and a vast quantity of them – 50,000 was the figure mentioned. They came from a medieval burial ground at York; the area was being cleared for building, and the local archaeological trust was excavating the site before the owners – Sainsbury's, just to make the meeting of worlds more piquant – buried the whole thing, presumably under a supermarket. End of first echo.

The bones came from graves which were believed to be, though the documents were not ample enough for anyone to be quite sure, those of Jews; the area in which the cemetery lay, near York, was called Jewbury. Second echo; our century has seen Jewish bones produced in quantities never attained in all previous history, though (third, ironical, echo) the massacre of Jews at York in the twelfth century had more than a touch of the murderous frenzy that raged in civilised Europe less than fifty years ago.

The archaeologists, who wished to study and measure the bones to see what could be discovered about the people to whom they belonged, consulted the Chief Rabbi, Sir Immanuel Jakobovits. After considering such evidence as the diggers had found, he asked them – and his wishes were at once met – to cease work on the examination of the bones and rebury them where they had been found. His reason was 'the reverence due to mortal remains which once bore the incomparable hallmark of the divine image, and which, we believe, have an inalienable right to stay undisturbed.' He added that 'dignity shown to human remains, even centuries after death, could contribute more than any scientific enquiry to human civilisation.'

Fourth echo: I have quoted the story from the pages of the *Guardian,* than which no newspaper today has a higher proportion of writers who would regard the Chief Rabbi's attitude as bizarre or perverse; I am sure, for instance, that Miss Polly Toynbee, who was recently waxing quite hysterical with relief at having found a nun who had not only left the convent but lost her faith on the way out, would not have the faintest idea of what the old boy was going on about, and for that matter precious little of what inspired the archaeologists' curiosity, her interest being limited to ensuring, when the Sainsbury's supermarket was erected on the site, that it would be amply stocked with muesli and unsweetened yoghurt, and that *foie gras* and South

African orange juice would be rigorously excluded from its shelves.

And yet it seems to me that something of great and enduring value in human civilisation is contained in the archaeologists' initial desire to examine the bones, in the Chief Rabbi's gently phrased appeal to them to desist, and in their ready willingness to relinquish their quest in what they recognised as a higher interest.

The archaeologists were driven by one of the noblest urges that civilised men and women can feel: the desire to join hands with the past and thus come closer to understanding both the past itself and what it can teach us about the present. When Schliemann sent his famous telegram, 'I have looked on the face of Agamemnon,' he was, as it transpired, mistaken; but the treasure he found at Mycenae was none the less far more valuable than the gold it was made of or the beauty of its workmanship, for it was a link with a story that has so far held captive the imagination of the world for twenty-eight centuries, and shows no sign at all of letting go.

So it was with Knossos, with Tutankhamun, with that amazing mosaic floor hard by Chichester, with the Ming Tombs of China, with every spadeful of earth carefully dug out of any archaeological site and examined carefully for evidence of the people who had preceded the diggers there, with Professor Glob and the bodies he kept finding, in a perfect state of preservation, beneath Denmark's watery soil, even with those splendid lunatics who burrowed their way into a hill beneath which they were convinced King Arthur was buried, and who emerged from the tunnel without Excalibur but with undiminished conviction.

I doubt if there is any such thing as a legend without some foundation in truth and history – no, not so much as Adam and Eve or Cinderella – and the desire to dig up even a single strand of evidence and patiently unravel it is one that should be, and is, admired by anybody with any imagination at all.

It is surely a measure of the York archaeologists' seriousness about their work that they so clearly understood and complied with the Chief Rabbi's wishes. All real archaeologists approach the past with the same attitude: reverence. The reverence is due to the past itself; if the diggers at York had found medieval kitchen utensils instead of bones they would have carried them no less carefully to their laboratory. But the reverence due to death, which was the Chief Rabbi's concern, intensifies the feeling of a meeting with the past, for it provides a link with a past that antedates the past itself, and must raise, in any mind not inextricably cntangled in the belief that *nothing* 'could contribute more than any scientific enquiry to human civilisation,' the question of why the dry bones once lived, and what breathed the life into them.

The reverence accorded to death is one of the oldest and most powerful ideas in human beings – so old, indeed, and so deeply embedded in so many societies, that it is hard to resist the conclusion that it must be biological; it would be as surprising to find an era or a culture that did not surround death with elaborate and profound beliefs and rituals as it would be to find a race of men with three legs. Some societies bury their dead, some burn them, some mummify and preserve them, some even eat them; all, however, start and finish with the same attitude, which is that in the presence of death we are as close as may be to solving the riddle of life, and it is therefore fitting that we should approach it in a spirit of awe. Why, of all the miracles, is it the raising of Lazarus that is the most powerful in its effect on our imagination and feelings? Because it cancelled the most uncancellable of debts, reversed the most irreversible of movements, denied the most palpable of proofs; if this man can annul death, then surely he is no man at all, and will one day annul his own.

So it is with the bones at York, and the

truth that the Chief Rabbi seized upon. There is an instinct in us all that he encapsulated when he spoke of 'the reverence due to mortal remains which once bore the incomparable hallmark of the divine image,' and added that 'the dignity shown to human remains' was a mark of true civilisation. One of the greatest terrors that haunts any deathbed is that of the casual or contemptuous disposal of the dying one's body. Our modern 'rationalists' would smile at something so primitive and superstitious as the belief that a dead body could matter to its previously living owner, and would never seek to enquire, however rationally, where the belief comes from, and why it is so strong. But that, after all, is why I have put 'rationalists' in quotation marks.

No one can now match a name or a face to a single bone of the great ossuary found at York. But it is not necessary to do so; it is necessary only to remember that those dead bones were once clad in flesh, and at once the mystery of life itself springs from the ground to confront us.

I saw a man die: he was a London bricklayer's labourer with seven children. He left seventeen pounds club money; and his wife spent it all on his funeral and went into the workhouse with the children next day. She would not have spent sevenpence on her children's schooling: the law had to force her to let them be taught gratuitously; but on death she spent all she had.

That passage is from *Man and Superman,* and it puts the opposite case very well. Those who know the play, however, will recall that the speaker is the Devil. The Chief Rabbi, and the York Archaeological Trust, know better, and those bones may now sleep soundly, undisturbed by the trolleys of Sainsbury's customers, until they wake never to sleep again.

The Times January 11th, 1984

15

Fight the good fight

There is a Church of England parish – let us call it, lest I should unwittingly add fuel to flames already liberally supplied therewith, by the name of the Reverend Alan Bennett's celebrated incumbency, St Jack-in-the-Lifeboat – in which all is not well between the shepherd and his flock.

The trouble began when the vicar proposed that the collection should be taken during the last hymn of the service, when, as he put it, 'the coin rattling and foot shuffling would be drowned.'

This, you may think, would be a logical step. The organist, however, saw it far otherwise; until now, the collection had always been taken during the sermon, and as far as he was concerned, it should continue to be. In the report of this unhappy business that I have seen, the organist is not quoted as drawing the appallingly obvious inference – that the drowning of the sermon in a sea of coin rattling and foot shuffling would be a less serious matter than the drowning of the accompaniment to a hymn – but none could deny that such an inference is hovering over the pulpit.

The vicar maintained his position, the organist his. Deadlock ensued, broken by the dismissal of the latter, presumably by the former. The vicar, it seemed, was at last in a position to deliver his sermons untroubled by the rattle of a single widow's mite or the shuffling of the smallest infant toe. The Hosts of Midian (or, depending which view of the matter you take, the Defenders of the Faith) were not, however, to be denied; the choir, all twenty of them, promptly downed psalters and came out on strike. This left

the vicar uninterrupted, but the inter-
ruptions unhymned; a new deadlock ensued, and the Bishop was called in. What
His Lordship said to the warring parties
history does not record, but shortly
afterwards the vicar went on holiday, the
organist was deemed 'suspended', and all
the Bishop would say for public con-
sumption was: 'The situation is a very
delicate one.'

I dare say, and made more so by a
disquieting new note struck by a
spokesman for the disaffected choir. 'The
vicar', he declared, 'is trying to introduce
high church practices here which we
dislike.'

Here I must make a personal dis-
claimer. I would rather put my head into
the mouth of a lion in the Roman arena
than get mixed up in a dispute over the
height of Christian church doctrine or
ritual; in these matters I am a paid-up,
card-carrying, lifelong Latitudinarian,
and a Jewish one to boot. I took no part
in the Reformation or Counter-Re-
formation, I have never been heard to

18

express a preference for *homoiousian* over *homoousian,* or vice versa, and anyone claiming to know my views on the place in Christian belief of confession, purgatory or candlesticks should be treated as an imposter. What is more, I am quite unable to see how the timing of the collection in a church could give rise to any question of orthodoxy or heterodoxy anyway, irrespective of the merits of the rival factions' claims to be the only guardians of the true faith.

But this makes me more, not less, confident of being able to pronounce upon the troubles at St Jack's. For whether the trouble there is concerned with the introduction of high church practices, or whether it is more in the nature of an industrial dispute, I have to tell the faithful to be not dismayed; it is quarrels of this kind, in parishes of this kind, which prove not only that the heart of the Anglican Church is still beating soundly in the body of the country it was born in, but that that country is itself still undamaged, unchanged and unsinkable.

'Rightly to be great,' said Hamlet,

> Is not to stir without great argument,
> But greatly to find quarrel in a straw,
> When honour's at the stake.

But the parishioners and clergy of that amazing institution, the Church of England, can and do find quarrel in a straw when *nothing's* at the stake, and those who believe that such an attitude shows that their church means nothing to them have got the matter upside down, inside out and back to front: it is precisely because they care so passionately for every blade of grass in the churchyard and every fold in the vicar's surplice that these weird and inexplicable dissensions arise among them, and it is because their faith is so deep and to them so clear, and therefore so rarely troubled by doctrinal dissension, that a disagreement over the best moment for the collection can turn into a battle of wills that splits the parish and leads to charges of high-handedness mingled with romanism and heresy. Come: is it not better for the choir to go on strike and the vicar to go on holiday than for both of them to go on an expedition in search of Albigensians to exterminate? Is it not better for the organist to cut the vicar dead than for him to pray to God to strike him dead? Is it not better for the Mothers' Union to bake loaves for the Harvest Festival than (as will soon be happening if some of our more *engagé* clergy have their way) to knit woollen hand-grenade covers for the Khmer Rouge?

We are, on the whole, an extraordinarily unwarlike and unexcitable nation. I believe that the failure of totalitarian political groups of both right and left to make headway with any substantial number of voters is only partly due to the voters' distaste for dictatorship and tyranny; it is also based on a profound and healthy abhorrence of systems which would inevitably entail Englishmen hitting other Englishmen over the head. Englishmen do, of course, hit other Englishmen over the head; but look why they do it. They do it in the course of quarrels about beer or football or one another's wives or, at the very worst, in the course of trying to steal one another's wallets. To suggest that they might take to doing it in the course of political disagreement would be regarded as a most outlandish idea, and the thought that they might do it in a religious cause would be incomprehensible to the point of embarrassment.

Long may it remain thus. The parishioners of St Jack-in-the-Lifeboat will be accused by the short-sighted of a failure in their sense of proportion. But surely they have displayed a sense of proportion of supreme delicacy and wisdom; they have quarrelled over things that do not matter, and have thus ensured that they will not be impelled to do each other harm, rather than – as with the Irish, to go no further for examples – over things that do matter, thus allowing themselves to be led into cursing one another's souls of murdering one another's bodies.

'If anyone speaks of religion in England,' said Montesquieu, 'everyone laughs.' That is perfectly true, but the Frenchman had missed the point. The laughter is directed at those who think it necessary to *speak* of religion, a practice to which foreigners are much given but which the English rightly think unnecessary. I will wager that even now they are not talking of religion in the streets of St Jack-in-the-Lifeboat. For what has happened there is that something disagreeable has been *injected into* the practice of their religion; the talk will be of organists and clergymen, choirs and collections, while beneath the talk their religion will continue to flow untroubled and unremarked. How the quarrel between the vicar and the choir is to be resolved I do not know; nor, apparently, does the Bishop. But we may be sure that the solution will be as English as the problem, and that not a drop of blood will be spilt in the course of it.

The Times June 20th, 1983

Scarlett runner

The road to Tara: The Life of Margaret Mitchell
by Anne Edwards*

What do *War and Peace* and *Gone with the Wind* have in common? Candidates less than fifty years of age should not attempt the question, as they have no chance of getting it right; for that matter, candidates more than fifty-five years old should not attempt it either, as they have no chance of getting it wrong.

These were the two books that the civilians of Britain read in the air-raid shelters, or behind their blacked-out bedroom windows, throughout the Second World War, and both admirably fulfilled

*Hodder and Stoughton, 1983.

the purpose for which they were bought in stupendous numbers. They are very long, so they lasted for months; they are set in the past, which took the readers' minds off the grim present; they are hugely colourful and romantic, which was fitting for a time when colour and romance were in short supply; they contain epic portraits of epic battles, which enabled those in mufti to identify with those who were fighting real epic battles elsewhere; they both hold the attention unflagging throughout their hundreds of thousands of words.

No doubt Tolstoy's is the better book, but its rival for the role of morale-booster to the Home Front did have the qualities I have outlined. And it had an extra advantage; the film of *Gone with the Wind* ran during the war in London (at the little Ritz Cinema, next door to the Empire) for nearly five years, which drove readers to see it and audiences to read the book. It is said that the usherettes eventually knew by heart, word for word, the entire four hours, before presumably being taken off to the funny-farm.

The readers of *War and Peace,* for some of whom it was the first book they had ever read, knew a little about Tolstoy, even if it was no more than that he was a Russian with a big bushy beard. Of the author of *Gone with the Wind,* however, nothing was known except the tittle-tattle, almost all of it untrue, to be found in the film magazines of the day. That in itself was astonishing, for the book had been, and still is, the greatest best-seller in history (the publishers, who had originally decided on a first printing of 10,000, had sold 100,000 before publication, and were to sell more than a million copies in the next six months, 50,000 of them in a single day), but perhaps it was just as well, for the readers of romantic novels like their authors to be romantic, too, and Margaret Mitchell, though there was something of Scarlett (originally called 'Pansy') in her, as there was a good deal of her first, disastrous husband in Rhett Butler, was very far indeed from the flawless porcelain figure the public longed for her to be. For one thing, she drank too much. For another, she was given to unladylike language and jokes.

No book about her was published before her death; indeed, she screamed blue murder, and threatened litigation, at the mere suggestion of a newspaper 'Profile'. She died (in a car accident she had predicted) in 1949, having left instructions that all her papers should be burned; they were, but her appeal to friends and other correspondents to destroy her letters was ignored by some of them, and gradually enough bits and pieces came to light for a biography. The first one was published in 1965; this is only the second.

Anne Edwards has been exceptionally assiduous in tracking down every scrap of information about the enigmatic author; assiduity, alas, has no effect on a prose style, and hers ('Lieutenant Henry loved to dance as much as Margaret did, and as they floated in each other's arms across the smooth floors of the Capital City

Club to the wispy strains of "Poor Butterfly" they were the centre of attention') gave me a vivid idea of what it would be like to be drowned in concentrated bubble-bath liquid.

Margaret Mitchell's horror of publicity, which in any case she could never quite disentangle from a contrary yearning for fame, did not spring from a desire to conceal a shameful past, or a least from a rational desire for such concealment. She was, however, quite hysterical about any mention of her first marriage (not without some justice, as 'Red' Upshaw kept drifting back into her life, and at one point apparently tried to rape her, and may even have succeeded), and hardly less so about the innocent details of her first romantic attachment. The sad truth is that she was clearly a confused and ultimately miserable woman, and could never wholly enjoy or wholly reject her success; though she was constantly dreaming of further literary projects, she never, in the end, wrote another book.

That was not really surprising; Miss

Edward's research emphasises how little Margaret Mitchell's life contained beside her one great triumph. Her tough, suffragette mother was of Huguenot stock, her father of Scottish; her maternal grandmother had been in Atlanta when it was burnt by Sherman. Margaret herself (she never grew beyond five feet) was a tomboy, repeatedly injured in riding accidents; she began to scribble as a child and although she dreamt of qualifying in medicine and becoming a psychiatrist she went – drifted, really – into journalism. She worked for years on *Gone with the Wind* before she would let anybody see it, and even then tried with some success to convince herself that she did not want it published.

It remains her monument. Though it is hardly to be ranked as great literature it is *not* pulp fiction; it paints a wholly credible portrait of the ancient South, romanticised to be sure but not invented, Margaret Mitchell took limitless pains to get every historical detail correct. But it is more than a daguerreotype; as Miss Edwards says:

> Perhaps the sales of a novel do not determine its literary qualifications, but its lasting images do. And who can now think of the South before, during, and after the Civil War without images drawn from the pages of *Gone with the Wind?*

And perhaps, in one sense, the sales of a novel *do* have some connection with its literary qualifications. The six million people who have bought it in hardback (200,000 copies were sold in Nazi Germany before the war!), were surely not wholly deceived, and surely it will be read when Harold Robbins and Irving Wallace and Frederick Forsyth are forgotten. No work that lasts can be wholly untrue to universal human experience, and any work that has something of universal human experience in it can make out a reasonable claim to be considered art. When the film was being made, Louis B. Mayer was told that it would run for four hours. His reply was 'They'd stone Christ if he came back and spoke for four hours.' For once, the master of giving the public what it wanted was wrong.

Observer July 17th, 1983

The saved and the just

The Last Jews in Berlin
by Leonard Gross*

Of all the by-products of the Holocaust, the story told in this book is perhaps the strangest and most pitiful. It concerns those German Jews who, from the beginning of Nazi rule to the end of the war and from the first disabilities heaped upon their people in the nascent Reich to the days of the Final Solution as the Gestapo roamed the streets looking for survivors to ship to Auschwitz, lived in hiding and, against fearful odds, survived.

Some lived rough; some got out of the

*Sidgwick and Jackson, 1983.

country through the heroic efforts of Swedish churchmen posted to wartime Germany; some, including the handful whose stories Mr Gross has chosen to tell in this book as representative, were hidden by courageous and honourable German Gentiles who risked their own lives to abide by Portia's rule:

Though justice be thy plea, consider this,
That in the course of justice none of us
Should see salvation: we do pray for mercy,
And that same prayer doth teach us all to render
The deeds of mercy.

One by one, as the terror closed in, Mr Gross's band of survivors, the 'U-boats', as such Jews called themselves (like U-boats they lived beneath the surface but had to take the risk of coming up from time to time), found refuge. The providers of the refuge were even more varied than the Jews they hid; from a blonde Aryan society beauty who was already working in the Resistance to a couple who were at first deeply reluctant to have anything to do with the Jews who sought their help, they shrugged and rose to giant human stature.

Much of the material in the survivors' accounts reads like the most lurid fiction, but the author, though this is a reporter's study rather than a scholar's, has checked everything that can be checked, and questioned both sheep and shepherds carefully; there can be no doubt that these stories are true not only in outline but in detail, including even the two cases of 'U-boats' who were betrayed and caught by the Gestapo but who managed to escape while waiting for the transports that were to take them to extermination, and to take up their underground life again where they had left off.

That word 'betrayed' covers the most terrible of all the darknesses in this book. There were Jews working for the Nazis as 'catchers'; they would prowl round areas where they knew Jews had formerly lived, or where they suspected they were being given refuge; if they spotted any of the U-boats coming up for air (and sometimes the refugees had not dared to venture out of doors for months on end) they would turn them in, sometimes using abominable trickery, to their enemies. We even know the names of two of them: Rolf Isaaksohn and Stella Kübler, and the latter, who served ten years in prison for her crimes, is still living in Berlin.

Some of the survivors, like the highly intellectual Hans Hirschel or the forceful and commanding Fritz Croner, had great inner resources that helped them to survive, but it is not as simple as that, for Willy Glaser had no such strength to fall back on; the only thing he knew was that he was irremediably mediocre (when he went underground he had no money, no papers and no idea what to do), yet he, too, came through.

None of them would have survived for

a week, of course, if it had not been for their benefactors, some of whom took horrifying risks to keep the hunted victims safe. For they needed not just hiding-places but food and identity-papers (which were necessary to obtain ration-cards), together with leak-proof stories for the neighbours to explain a strange face behind the curtains. The protector's attitude was summed up by Joseph Wirkus, one of those who were at first unwilling to get involved, protesting that the refugees could only stay briefly, and ended by not only hiding them for years but by adding other refugees until the house was bursting with them: at each step that led inevitably to another and more dangerous step, Wirkus would intone 'We have said A, now we must say B', and marched stolidly on down his logical and heroically generous path.

Perhaps even more remarkable was the actions of many of the shepherds' neighbours; it eventually transpired that almost all the sheepfolds were surrounded by people who knew perfectly well what was going on, but who, though they did not dare to go so far as to shelter refugees themselves, never betrayed them. There was even a Gestapo officer who, in the course of an interrogation and under the nose of his brother-interrogator, managed to drop a life-saving hint.

This book tells the story of those who were not caught, those who were (and whose benefactors must have died with them) were not in a position to answer the author's questions. Estimates vary of the numbers of Jews who survived in the capital of a regime sworn to kill them; perhaps a few thousand, perhaps only a few hundred. Mr Gross's group remained in Berlin after the war ended and made new lives for themselves; two of the men married their shepherdesses; perhaps even Willy Glaser was not as mediocre as he thought.

The book is another nail in the coffin of the Manichee; the reader takes from it a vivid and enduring memory of goodness on the part of the saviours while the evil of the persecutors, though omnipresent, remains the backdrop to the drama. Truly, death shall have no dominion; Abraham's plea that the Lord should spare the cities of the plain if fifty righteous men should be found there would certainly have served to save Berlin.

Observer August 7th, 1983

Will the real Vermeer please stand up?

L ast week a Manet was sold at Christie's in New York for $4 million. The same auction house, it is announced, is to sell in London some of the works of Mr Tom Keating, including pictures bearing his own signature as well as ones more imaginatively signed with names such as Titian and Rembrandt. (Reader, do not leap to conclusions; these may be perfectly genuine paintings by Nigel Titian and Kevin Rembrandt – artists less well known than their namesakes, perhaps, but not to be condemned out of hand for that).

The first thing to be said is not the most important, but it might as well be said nevertheless: it is that I wouldn't half laugh if the Manet turned out to be by Mr Keating too. I shall not dwell upon the well-known disparity between what great artists of the past earned for their work and what dealers in those works now make out of them, because in the first place the argument is too worn, and in the second place it is largely spurious anyway, being usually employed for de-nunciations of the consumer society by artists who couldn't draw a triangle, never mind a real picture. Anyway, D. B. Wyndham Lewis said the last word from that point of view a long time ago:

> Manet made so little monet,
> Dealers thought it rather fonet;
> As for Monet, some (not manet)
> Thought he wasn't making anet.

But this brings me back to a question that has haunted me for decades. Readers old enough to remember who van Meegeren was must bear with me while I remind the rest.

He was a Dutch art dealer and minor artist, who remained in the Netherlands throughout the Second World War and German Occupation, following his trade as best he could. After the war, he was prosecuted as a collaborator, the evidence being that he had sold to Goering a masterpiece by Vermeer, a huge 'Christ at Emmaus'. The picture was undoubtedly among Goering's loot, and it had certainly been sold to him or his agents by van Meegeren, so the case looked black. The dealer, however, pleaded not guilty, and his defence caused a considerable sensation. He claimed that instead of being condemned for collaborating with the enemy he should be commended for making fools of them, for, so far from the picture being by Vermeer, he had painted it himself.

His claim was greeted with considerable scepticism; the picture had been vouched for by leading art experts. Whereupon, Van Meegeren caused an even greater sensation; he announced that if the court would order him to be provided in his prison with canvas, brushes, paint and a sufficiency of north light he would be pleased to match the customer's sample by turning out another Vermeer on the same scale and with the same apparent authenticity. And that is precisely what he did. (When he did it, the Dutch authorities behaved shabbily, they prosecuted van Meegeren for forgery, and he was sentenced to a year in prison, where he died. Now I come to think of it, the British authorities behaved just as badly to the memorably named Mr Kempton Bunton, who stole the Goya 'Duke of Wellington' but later returned it unharmed. They prosecuted him for stealing the frame, which he had not returned, and he, too was imprison- ed. It is always dangerous, it seems, to make fools of the foolish).

Now for van Meegeren's Question. As it happens, he did not ask it himself, though it enshrined what was obviously his view; it occured in a play about the case, at one point in which van Meegeren is reflecting on the fact that his 'Christ at Emmaus' was universally accepted as genuine until he himself proved that it was a fake. I quote van Meegeren's Question from memory, but it went something like this:

> Yesterday, this picture was worth millions of guilders, and experts and art-lovers would come from all over the world and pay money to see it. Today, it is worth nothing, and nobody would cross the street to set it free. *But the picture has not changed.* What has?

I am blowed if I know, and the unblowed are warned that any attempt to provide the question with a snap answer will certainly come to grief. (Suppose, for instance, that van Meegeren had died before his trial; his Vermeer would presumably be accepted to this day. Moreover, he was able to get away with the original sale because there is evidence that Vermeer did paint such a picture, which had been presumed lost. So suppose that van Meegeren had died without revealing his secret, and the real Vermeer had then turned up; how would the experts have adjudicated between the two, and how would they have convinced anybody that they had made the right decision, whatever it was? Or suppose van Meegeren had left, to be opened after his death, a statement that his defence had been bogus, and that the disputed picture had been genuine after all? And suppose that that had happened, and the *genuine* genuine one had been found, and the experts had divided into two equal camps of supporters – which one would we have paid good money to see and be impressed by?)

The price of a picture is determined by supply and demand, within a framework of fashion, so there is no clue there; certainly some people will go to see a picture that has been sold for a record sum just *because* of the money it fetched, but they would also go to see, for the same reason, a giant uncut diamond or for that matter a very large pile of banknotes. The beauty of a picture ought not to be in the eye of the beholder, but that 'ought' is a fat lot of use in the face of van Meegeren's success, and for that matter a fat consolation for those who bought (and sold) Mr Keating's Palmers. If we stood in front of van Meegeren's Vermeer and felt profoundly affected by the majesty and power of the scene, just why would we stop feeling such things if a newsboy rushed into the gallery shouting that it had just been proved a fake?

Well, let me step into the witness-box myself. I have just published a book, in one chapter of which I go rattling on for pages about Vermeer's 'The Servant Pouring Milk' in the Rijksmuseum; I have gazed upon that picture countless times, for many hours in all, but I simply do not know what I would feel on my next visit if before it took place the picture was conclusively proved to be by Mr Denis Skinner, Lord Chief Justice Lane, or Mr Clive James.

If I would feel the same as I always

have, then the identity of the artist is not important. In one sense, that is obviously true: there are some very great pictures which have never been attributed to any known artist. But suppose Mr Skinner, the LCJ or Mr James had been shown to have painted the picture, deliberately, in the style of Vermeer, which is what van Meegeren did: why would the authorship then start to matter – to matter so much, indeed, that I might no longer feel the same about it?

It is no use saying that there is a vast gulf between any masterpiece and any imitation of it, however meticulous. I have no doubt there is, but if we cannot see the difference – and successful art forgery would not exist if we could – what exactly does the difference consist of, apart from the fact that there must be one? Suppose that that four-million-dollar Manet did turn out to be a fake: the buyer could get his money back from Christie's, of course, but questions of legal liability plainly have nothing to do with artistic validity, so what would then be the standing of the oohs and ahs – quite genuine ones, I am sure – heard in the saleroom when it was held up before the bidding started?

Then again, what about a picture that has hung, neglected, in the corner of a gallery, for many years, attributed to a minor follower of Raphael? All of a sudden the greatest Raphael expert in the world takes a good look at it, and declares that it is from the master's own hand: all other experts look at it and agree, and the queues begin to form. Never mind the *motives* of the queuers: what has caused the difference in their *feelings* in front of the picture, which have changed overnight from casual interest to passionate devotion? (Remember van Meegeren: 'The picture has not changed. What has?')

The horrid truth seems to be that our response to art rests on a foundation much less secure than we like to think. I suppose it begins when we begin to learn about art, and all too often to learn about it in terms of hierarchies of eminence, so that Rembrandt = good is an equation fixed in our minds forever. But it is all too easy to believe, and millions do believe it, that his paintings are good because he is Rembrandt; in fact, his paintings are good because of the qualities to be found in them, and they would be no less good if they were by Smith, Jones or Anon, yet the result of the equation-learning (the equivalent of the 'capes and bays' method of teaching geography when my mother was a girl) is that many visitors to an art gallery look first for the label which tells them who painted it, and then at the picture to see not what is there but what the label has told them.

If Rembrandt is good, then we are obliged to experience the appropriate response when looking at a picture he painted, and if we fail to experience it we are obliged to keep quiet. Conversely, when we are looking at a picture by not-Rembrandt, we accept that we are forbidden to feel the response appropriate to his work. Now: what happens when we are looking at a Rembrandt, with the right feelings, and we are told that it is a fake? The answer, surely, is the answer to van Meegeren's question: we switch off the feeling at once, and switch on the feeling appropriate to fakes – that is, an indignation made the more intense by the realisation that we have been fooled.

I have to say that I have never felt quite so tentative in offering an answer to a question in my life. But if that, or something like it, is not the answer to van Meegeren's riddle, what is? I think I had better leave it there, retreating in good order under the cover provided by Beachcomber's account of Captain Foulenough's brief career as the owner of a shady art gallery where hacks turned out rubbishy daubs which were then sold to credulous millionaires as examples of the finest modern art. One evening, Foulenough got drunk and signed a hideous abstract 'Tintoretto'. Even the sucker who was to be bamboozled into buying it jibbed at this, and the captain, thinking fast, insisted that the signature was in fact that of *Tintoretto*, an artist in the most *avant* of *gardes*. Thus reassured, the sucker paid up, and presumably van Meegeren, from that corner of Heaven reserved for those who have smitten the Philistines with the jawbone of an ass, chuckled quietly. My compliments to Tom Keating, and if he will only claim publicly to have painted the Manet there will be a bottle of champagne waiting for him *chez* Levin as soon as he cares to call.*

The Times November 24th, 1983

*Mr Keating wrote to me, generously disclaiming any hand in the Manet. Shortly afterwards, alas, he died.

Thoughts on a cold pavement

It was five minutes past curtain-time, and I was beginning to wonder (knowing that at this particular theatre they tend to be punctual in starting) whether all was not well with the leading lady, when a familiar figure appeared in front of the curtain and said, with a kind of authoritative charm, 'Ladies and gentlemen, I'm afraid we have a rather special kind of problem this evening, and we must ask you to leave the building at once – the police will notify you when you may return.'

We rose, and proceeded in an orderly fashion to the exits. (Two members of the audience were seen *running,* but it was agreed by the rest of us that they must have been foreigners). In the hour or so we spent on the pavement in weather that would have frozen a penguin, it was possible to reflect on certain questions of the day in a particularly concentrated manner.

First, it was noticeable that nobody at all was in doubt as to the meaning of the management's words, though 'bomb', 'telephone-call' and 'danger' were not among them. Second, nobody grumbled, except at the perishing cold; those who might be presumed to have caused us our discomfort were not abused *in absentia,* nor was there any sense of outrage. Nobody even denounced the management for shutting the cloakrooms as soon as the evacuation order was decided upon, and nobody ventured the opinion that they should have treated the telephone-call as the hoax it was overwhelmingly likely (and in the event proved) to be.

Next, it was apparent once more that

an emergency always brings out the friendliness in the British; people who had never met before were talking to each other within a few minutes, and I daresay that in years to come there will be devoted couples telling their friends 'We met in a bomb-scare.' (Kenneth Tynan, reviewing *The Iceman Cometh,* said that in the fourth hour the atmosphere in the theatre was exactly like that in a wartime air-raid shelter, with 'complete strangers offering one another wine-gums').

And finally, I had the melancholy and useless satisfaction of knowing that I solved this problem some years ago, and publicly announced my solution, too, though I did not expect anything to be done (nor was it), because the people who would have had to do the doing were those in charge of the telephone service; I have no expectation that British Telecom will be any more heedful than their predecessors, but I may as well repeat my solution anyway. It is to change from our present telephone system of what is technically known as

'Calling party release' to 'Called party release.' At present if I call you and you hang up but I don't, you remain connected to me; if the system were inverted, the bomb-hoaxer (or genuine bomb planter for that matter) would hang up, having given his ominous message, only to find that he was still connected to his victim, thus enabling him to be traced promptly and with certainty.

Meanwhile, a few conclusions can be drawn. It is little more than a decade since serious urban terrorism in civilised Western societies began; before that, there was nothing to worry about, apart from the internecine wars of Chicago gangsters, a brief flurry by the IRA just before the Second World War, and the random actions of those who were collectively known as anarchists and who were so little regarded as a threat to society that the type was always portrayed as a comic figure with a cloak, a fringe beard, and a round 'infernal machine' which was gently smoking and invariably labelled 'Bomb'.

Nous avons changé tout cela. And yet ...
Air piracy is of the same modernity as
bomb-planting, but we no more grumble
at, or find in any way surprising, the
searches of luggage and person at
airports than we get hysterical, or even
seriously cross, when we are turned out
of a theatre. Every now and again a real
bomb goes off in a city far removed from
areas of endemic political violence; unless it causes large numbers of casualties
(particularly among horses) it now makes
hardly a ripple across the public consciousness. Baader-Meinhof Gangs, Red
Army Factions, Weathermen – they
have killed people from time to time, but
not more, I imagine than are struck by
lightning, or indeed are accounted for by
the Charles Mansons and Dennis Nilsens
and their like. (There are as many
'ordinary' murders in Los Angeles in a
single year as there have been corpses in
Northern Ireland attributable to terrorism since the present 'Troubles' began).

Of course, the hoaxers have battened
on the activities of the killers in a manner

which is unique to our time, and there must be dozens of false alarms to every real emergency. That makes life more troublesome, as those who went wheezing about their business the day after our pavement vigil in the cold could testify; if it comes to that, there were, no doubt, people who had to leave before the end of the performance to catch their last trains and buses, though if the curtain had gone up on time they could have stayed to the end.

What does all that amount to? A few horrible deaths and injuries; a far greater quantity of inconvenience patiently and light-heartedly borne (when the 'sniffer' dogs arrived – gentle-looking Labradors – and lolloped into the theatre as into a Disney cartoon, they were greeted by laughter rather than cheers); and, surely, the defeat, almost total, of the enemy.

Are lives seriously disrupted or made less worth living by such trivia? In Lebanon, life must be hardly bearable; in Belfast it must be at least very different; but I am not talking of the centres of violence, only of the violence in those countries where it is either random (as in West Germany and Italy) or designed (as in mainland Britain) to bring pressure to bear on those who will ultimately have to decide whether the centres of violence can be pacified by political action.

The truth that emerges is very encouraging. First in the United States, then in Western Germany, then increasingly in Italy, the political urban terrorists have been reduced to tiny handfuls of disheartened wretches. They have been reduced by patient, unwavering work on the part of democratic authorities and their forces of order, and by the refusal of the general public either to panic or to demand that peace should be achieved by surrender.

There was neither fear nor anger on that chilly pavement the other night; only an instinctive understanding that the price we were paying to keep our society not only free but calm and ordered was ludicrously small compared to what it was buying. If the hoaxer who turned us out into the night is caught, I think six months or so in the hoosegow would be appropriate, besides tending to discourage others like him, for it is not actually *fun* to freeze to death even if everybody around you is freezing to death as well. But if we have to waste a few minutes at an airport, or get cold outside a theatre once a year, or even be startled from time to time by a loud bang followed by the sound of fire-engines and ambulances, civilised life will not become impossible, or even by seriously diminished. And even if we have to put up with those things for decades to come, that will remain true. Why, when in the interval of the resumed performance I met the spokesman who had made the original ominous announcement, I shook his hand warmly, in token that all was forgiven. And in truth there was nothing to forgive.

The Times December 9th, 1983

Love's state secrets

H. H. Asquith: Letters to Venetia Stanley
edited by Michael and Eleanor Brock*

One Sunday morning in the early spring of 1912, Herbert Asquith, who was then sixty years old and had been Prime Minister for four years (he was to hold the office for four more), fell totally in love, in a single instant, with Venetia Stanley, one of his daughter Violet's friends and contemporaries, thirty-five years his junior. Or so it is said, not least by him, and since in the course of the following thirty-four months he wrote her at least 560 letters, almost every single one of which pours out love and adoration in

*Oxford, 1982.

59

terms unqualified by any apparent re-
collection that he was a married man as
well as Prime Minister, my claim that I
don't believe a word of it may seem –
indeed, may *be* – difficult to sustain.

The evidence is certainly formidable.
In the first four months of 1915 alone he
wrote 186 letters to Venetia: sometimes
there were three in a day, and on occasion
four. He wrote them from his country
house, from 10 Downing Street, from
trains and motor-cars, from the houses of
his friends, from the Front Bench of the
House of Commons, from the Cabinet
Room *while the Cabinet was in session,* under
the noses of his hostesses, his colleagues,
his opponents and his wife.

His recklessness in the affair (it was
apparently never consummated, and
from the tone of his letters it seems very
unlikely that the thought of a physical
relationship ever crossed his mind)
suggests that he was not simply drunk on
love (or liquor – he did have a drink
problem) but deranged; from the outbreak of the Great War he was sending

her the most secret military information, much of which, in enemy hands, could have led directly to the rout and slaughter of British troops, and most of these letters went by ordinary post.

When the letters begin Asquith was in the throes of the struggle over Home Rule; he and his Government, unable to square the circle, faced the certainty of civil war in Ireland (Redmond takes on a greater stature through the evidence of these extraordinarily candid documents, and Carson becomes even more repugnant), from which he and the Liberals were saved only by the outbreak of war in Europe – one of the greatest ironies of all the irony-strewn history of Anglo-Irish relations.

Even as early as Letter 31 his indiscretion was astounding: he was, for instance, eager to send her in advance the crucial paragraph about Home Rule from the King's Speech in February 1914, and only refrained because she expressed no interest in it. 'There is nothing (as you know)', he wrote, 'that I would not show you: so great and deep is my trust.' (There is no evidence that she ever betrayed it).

In effect, these letters constitute Asquith's detailed, intimate political diary, day by day and sometimes hour by hour. They thus constitute a source-book of British history for the period covered that will be of enormous and enduring value, and the story they tell, public and private, is of the most enthralling nature; readers in a hurry are warned that for all its 600 pages the book is impossible to skip.

There are wonderfully vivid portraits of the politicians and others around him: Churchill, impetuous, dashing, obstinate; the creepy Simon (Asquith calls him 'Sinless John' or 'the Impeccable'); Lloyd George, up to his neck in conspiracies; Arnold Bennett, 'a bounder of the first degree'; Kitchener, who was plainly half mad, and Jacky Fisher, who was at least three-quarters so (he wanted to shoot all the German prisoners-of-war in Britain); and the Jewish Edwin

Montagu, 'the Assyrian' to Asquith, who courted Venetia before the period of the correspondence, resumed his suit towards its end (at least once they were both writing to her during the same Cabinet meeting, and Montagu even complains that Winston won't shut up long enough for him to finish the letter) and emerged victorious, breaking Asquith's heart in the process. (He thought Montagu unworthy of Venetia, not least, apparently, because he was a Jew.)

Even at the height of the Irish crisis, the Austrian ultimatum to Serbia that led to the war, the chaos in the early days of the BEF and the retreat from Mons, the Dardanelles tragedy itself, Asquith, recording history and his feelings together, wrote steadily on, as indeed he played relentlessly on at bridge and even golf; the flavour of a vanished world in which there was always enough time is beautifully conveyed. So is the strength he found in Venetia:

It has been given I suppose to few

men to go through such a succession of 'crises' in the same space of time; you have been a stay and refreshment to me in them all; and during this last 12 months with its almost miraculous series of emergencies I have come more and more to rely and rest upon you, and you have never failed me either in counsel or in love.

How much he depended on her is made clear from the profound depressions into which he fell if the post was late or, even worse, if there was no letter from her in it.

But love? Certainly he believed that that was what he felt:

My love for you has grown day by day and month by month and (now) year by year: till it absorbs and inspires all my life. I could not if I would, and would not if I could, arrest its flow, or limit its extent, or lower by a single degree its intensity, or make it a less sovereign and dominating factor in

my thoughts and purposes and hopes
. . . It enables me in the daily stress of
almost intolerable burdens and
anxieties to see visions and dream
dreams. . . .

Now those are surely the words of a
man in love not with a woman but with
an idealised *feeling* of love; as the tide of
words mounts higher it becomes plain
that the whole thing is a beautiful
construction, built on a real foundation
(of his need for a confidante) but having
no more substance than any cloud-
capped tower or insubstantial pageant
that leaves not a wrack behind.

Asquith, as he says himself, saw
visions and dreamed dreams; though I
am unable to believe in them, they give
a strange and hauntingly ethereal quality
to a fascinating and massively detailed
account of the last days of Liberal
England, and of the man who presided
over the end of a world. Venetia stares
out from the jacket, a cool beauty with
marvellous eyes; any reader of this

tremendous book will feel forever indebted to her for inspiring it.

Observer November 28th, 1982

Exit to the unthinkable

The arguments, legal and ethical, over the Voluntary Euthanasia Society and its activities will not end with the court case recently concluded. Miss Gillian Tindall, a few days later, put the case, on this page, for the Voluntary Euthanasia Society and its wish to disseminate information that will help intending suicides to achieve their aim. Now I propose to put the cae against it.

I must first draw attention to the title of the society's do-it-yourself suicide manual; it is called *A Guide to Self-Deliverance*. This rich and striking example of Newspeak suggests that the society's leaders are by no means so sure of themselves as they would like to think, let alone as they would like *us* to think. The booklet, after all, as is admitted by the society (it is not available to non-members, or even to members under twenty-five), gives advice to those who wish to commit suicide; it would surely be better, therefore, to call it *A Guide to Suicide* or, even more plainly and honestly, *How to Kill Yourself.* This question of nomenclature is not the most important, but it is not at all unimportant, and should be borne in mind; 'Self-Deliverance' in this context is a sanitised word, a perfumed word, an advertiser's or vendor's word, and we have the right to ask why it was used.

Miss Tindall, in her article, quoted a remark made by one of the counsel in the legal proceedings, presumably counsel for the defendants; he spoke of 'the sovereign, unalienable and absolute right to die.' That, clearly, is the heart of the argument, and I shall return to it, but first there are some other matters to get out of the way.

Suicide is no longer a crime; it used to be the one offence on the Statute Book that was punishable only if it was unsuccessful, which was widely portrayed as absurd, but obviously the point of the criminal law was to put a barrier before those who would help others to kill themselves (the survivor of a suicide pact was sometimes prosecuted), which was anything but absurd in view of the danger that, for instance, elderly and inconvenient relatives might be steered, not altogether with their approval, in a direction from which they would not return.

At this point it must be said that the Voluntary Euthanasia Society certainly does not need me to draw to its attention the dangers of which I have given one example; it is fully cognisant of them, and has proposed practical ways to minimise them. What it cannot do, however, is to predict the consequences of legalising, not suicide (which is already legal), but any form, however controlled and safeguarded, of helping to their deaths individuals who wish to die but are unable, say by reason of physical disability, to commit suicide unaided. (This was, of course, the central theme of Mr Brian Clark's successful play *Whose Life Is It Anyway?*)

But if there are rigid and inescapable safeguards in any such proposals, what untoward conequences can there be? In the answer to that lies one of the most terrible truths about mankind. Once we legalise assisted suicide we have altered, significantly and irrevocably, the stand-point from which we observe such matters, and once we have done that, things which were previously quite unthinkable move into an area in which it is possible to think them. And having been thought, sooner or later they, too, will be proposed. No reader of these words needs me to say precisely what I am talking about, but the Fallacy of the Altered Standpoint is the sign-manual of our bloodstained century, and I do not believe that the smallest countenance should be given to suggestions, no matter how scrupulous, sensible and reputable their advocacy, which would give any further credence to that fallacy.

All this, however, concerns the social and legal aspects of suicide, and these, though important, do not constitute the essence of the real question, which is: was Hamlet right when he said that the Almighty had fixed his canon 'gainst self-slaughter?

It should be noted first that almost all of the great religions set their face against suicide; for Roman Catholics it is a sin even to contemplate it (Dante puts the suicides in the seventh circle of Hell). Nor is it difficult to see why this should be so; all religions teach in one way or another, that our lives are not ours but God's, and may not, therefore, be thrown away. But does it make sense to argue that suicide is wrong for those who have no religious beliefs to restrain them?

Here we must tread carefully. I suppose most people have known suicides; a surprisingly large number have known suicides; a surprisingly large number have contemplated taking their own lives. Who are we to judge, say, those who are suffering from some incurable and agonising disease, or who face some other insupportable misery or loss, and anticipate the inevitable by their own hand? Well, of course I do not judge them, in the sense of condemning or censuring them; but is it impossible to say that they may be mistaken in their belief that they have that 'sovereign, unalienable and absolute right'?

To begin with there is the extra-ordinary and surely meaningful fact the *nothing* is hopeless. There is no 'incurable' disease known to medicine that is without its cases of spontaneous remission, no bereavement so cruel that it can never be accepted and survived, no disgrace so total that it cannot be lived through. In every category of suicide there have been those who, with the same overwhelming justification, have stayed their hands, and not regretted it. (We have no means of knowing how many of those who have not stayed their hands have regretted it too late). Second, there is the no less extraordinary and meaningful fact that the life instinct is the most powerful and tenacious in human kind. Consider the unending and hopeless privations, tortures, degradations, that men and women have survived, solely because of the limitless strength of the determination to stay alive – a determination which sometimes works far below a consciousness that cries out to die. Look at that most haunting image of our time, that crowd of living skeletons in the liberated concentration camps who, by all imaginable tests, should have long previously given up the fight to live, yet who insisted on staying alive for a dawn they had no reason to believe would ever come. Look at the injuries that the human body had sustained and survived, the poverty and hunger, the rejection and hatred; why, even John Merrick, the 'elephant man', who could not possibly have foreseen the unique accident that saved him, did not take his own life, despite a condition among the most terrible it has been given to a human being to endure.

'Given'; have I begged the question, or instinctively answered it? I am one of those – and we are many today – who, without any definable set of religious beliefs, yet cannot persuade themselves that life is an accident, the universe random, and both without ultimate meaning. If life has meaning, derived from a universe that itself makes sense, then we surely have a duty to use all the life that we have, to accept, and to learn from, whatever may befall us, to ignore or reject nothing, to believe that understanding and enlightenment may come to us between the stirrup and the ground, or indeed in the very moment of death. But until that moment, I believe that we must carry the vessel of life over even the stoniest ground without deliberately spilling it, and history is full of men and women who have obeyed that command whatever the cost. Am I not right in believing that there is only one suicide in the New Testament? If I am, I hardly think I need tell you his name.

The Times May 5th, 1983

Speaking in tongues

Daphne into Laurel: Translation of Classical Poetry from Chaucer to the Present
edited by Richard Stoneman*

It is possible to learn a great deal about one country from the way it translates the literature of another, and indeed from its choice of what foreign literature to translate. Almost all French Shakespeare, for instance, is bad, including the Gide *Hamlet,* and it is bad because the French literary tradition is so un-Shakespearian that the translators have generally been quite unable to take his measure. Similarly, the strangeness of Goethe is

*Duckworth, 1982.

precisely the kind of strangeness that bemuses the anglophone mind; I have never yet come across a really satisfactory *Faust* in English, and I do not expect to.

Latin and Greek literature provides the perfect test, first because all Western literature is steeped in it, and second because every age has translated it afresh, so that we can watch, through this serviceable prism, a nation's mind unfolding over the centuries. Mr Stoneman's anthology is comprehensive and informatively and carefully edited (apart from a shocking misquotation of Wordsworth); he tips his hat to Chaucer and ends with C. H. Sisson and Ted Hughes, but the bulk of his collection comes, as one would expect, from the sixteenth, seventeenth and eighteenth centuries. He has mercifully omitted most of the merely worthy (Beerbohm drew a cartoon of a 'Statesman of the Olden Time, making without wish for emolument a flat but faithful version of the Georgics in English hexameters') but rightly includes a few examples of the downright dreadful, such as the Homer of Arthur Hall, published about 1590, which includes the memorable line 'Nine days throughout right brave they feast, the banquets were not bad.'

Most of the greatest English poets before modern times essayed classical translation (itself a comment on the changing place of the classics in this country's education), and at times practically every poet in the land: Mr Stoneman says of the seventeenth century that 'by the Restoration, translation was nothing short of a craze.'

Latin, on the whole, preceded Greek; English Hellenism is a fairly late flower. Chapman's Homer appeared when the argument over metre was at its height, and men went to battle for the hexameter as fiercely as Don Quixote for Dulcinea. His use of the dangerously cumbersome fourteener for the *Iliad* (published first) proved an *ignis fatuus* for some who followed, and he abandoned it himself in the *Odyssey,* for the pentameter, which on the whole has carried the day.

We all know what Keats felt on first looking into Chapman's Homer; but what did he find there? He found not only a great poet engaging his mind with that of another, but a man of his time who used Homer as a mirror, and saw his own and his time's face in it. It is obvious in the case of some translators that their achievements could stand independent of the original; a reader who had never heard of Homer would not deduce his existence from Chapman, and still less from Pope. The editor is severe on Bentley's 'A very pretty poem, Mr Pope, but you must not call it Homer,' but the fact remains that it must *not* be called Homer, because Homer was not an eighteenth-century Englishman writing and thinking in the atmosphere that surrounded him and without any great desire to escape it.

It Chapman and Pope are the greatest examples of the translator who produces an 'original', the finest of those who have, consciously or unconsciously, tried to keep an ancient mind in a modern body is surely Dryden; a mere four lines from his Lucretius will show his power:

> What has this bugbear death to frighten man,
> If souls can die, as well as bodies can?. . .
> From sense of grief and pain we shall be free,
> We shall not feel, because we shall not be.

Homer, Virgil, Horace and Ovid have provoked the greatest number of translators, which is only to be expected; Catullus has brought more to grief than any other poet, which is likewise unremarkable, for translating Catullus is like singing Mozart – there is nowhere to hide. The more credit to Abraham Cowley, no great servant of the muses in his own right, for a delightful and almost wholly successful version of 'Acme and Septimius', which ends thus:

> If the Gods would please to be

But advis'd for once by me,
I'de advise 'em when they spie
Any illustrious piety,
To reward her, if it be she
To reward him, if it be he;
With such a husband, such a wife,
With Acme's and Septimius' life.

I wish Mr Stoneman had included more versions of the same passages by different hands; we have Milton and Landor competing in one Horatian Ode, and Congreve and Allan Ramsay in another, but that is all. The Ramsay is an astonishing achievement, reminding me of Henley's dazzling success with Villon's 'Tout aux tavernes et aux filles', which he turned into the equivalent English thieves' argot ('Booze and the blowens cop the lot'); it is pure Burns, and in places needs another translation, but I finished it wanting to cheer:

Guid claret best keeps out the cauld,
An' drives awa' the winter soon;
It makes a man baith gash an' bauld,

An' heaves his saul ayont the
moon...

Her laugh will lead you to the place
Where lies the happiness you want,
An' plainly tells you to your face,
Nineteen nay-says are hauf a grant.

Herrick at translation sounds almost
more like Herrick than Herrick in
his own voice; Johnson hardly comes to
life; Bulwer-Lytton turns in a surprisingly good Horace; William Morris,
anachronistic to the last, returns to the
fourteener; the Browning Version, for all
Mr Stoneman's defence of it, is terrible;
Gladstone and Swinburne rub shoulders
uneasily; I find more in Pound's trans-
lations than ever I have in his own work;
Gilbert Murray survives all attempts
(including Eliot's) to overthrow him.

Observer January 9th, 1983.

Ars longa, Booker brevis

I think we had better straighten out our ideas about literature, publication, book prizes and book promotion. There has of late been much high-minded comment about such enterprises as the '12 Best Post-War Novels' and the Booker prize; Mr Christopher Booker (no relation) was speaking for such views a few days ago when he wrote that:

> The publishing and bookselling trade has never been so geared to producing vast quantities of glossily packaged, frenetically publicized books, the great majority of which . . . are little more

than rubbish ... Most of those engaged in 'the book business' have been swept up into a self-deluding charade which has ... little to do with the real merits of literature ....

At the same time Mr Nicholas de Jongh, taking a welcome break from his normal weekly announcement that the Royal Shakespeare Company is about to close down for lack of funds, devoted himself to a theme nowadays heard at least as frequently as Mr Booker's; he declared that the Arts Council's Literature Department, Marghanita Laski up, has failed the nation and must go, adducing as his evidence that:

There could be no more damning testimony to the literature department's creative bankruptcy than the fact that for the last two financial years ... the department failed to spend a considerable portion of its grant allocation ... In the last two years it has focused attention on the encouragement of readers rather than writers . . .

On the face of it, the argument espoused by the high-minded Booker (who writes on vellum in an unheated monk's cell with a signed photograph of Aristotle on the wall before him) is the very opposite of that put forward by the low-minded de Jongh (who writes at Langan's Brasserie on a word-processor lightly sprinkled with Beaujolais Nouveau). The one is appalled at the publication and boosting of 'non-books by non-authors'; the other is so eager for more authors to get their bread in the gravy that he condemns the Arts Council for withholding bursaries from the authors of 'indifferent work' – presumably Booker's 'non-books by non-authors.' Booker condemns the 'seedy mediocrity' of his namesake prize, and deplores the 'huge, fraudulent structure' of the publicity machine; de Jough calls for a Literature Trust to 'seek out serious writers far more successfully than the

Literature Department has managed' – no doubt with the aid of Booker's 'huge, fraudulent structure' – and denounces the 'lofty elitists' who have neglected such essential seeking, presumably with the applause of Booker.

Yet it seems to me that both of these critics of the present state of affairs are trapped in the same fallacy. They assume that literature is a plant as frail and endangered as the darling buds of May and that it can flourish only if the right conditions – more money in de Jongh's view, less vulgarity in Booker's – are present; they also believe that whatever the right conditions are they can be brought into being by the actions of the right people.

When the Decca Record Company made its historic first recording of *The Ring,* the BBC in turn made a television programme about its making. *The Songwriter's Guild News* protested at the lavishing of such resources on such a work, and asked indignantly: 'Can the BBC find no British work of comparable stature to film? If not, surely they could have commissioned one.'

To be sure, that is a somewhat extreme form of missing the point, but in principle the writer was doing the same as Messrs Booker and de Jongh (and for that matter Fay Weldon, whose speech at the Booker Prize award dinner managed to combine both of their approaches). For you see, a publisher – or a Literature Trust, or an Arts Council, or for that matter a committee of angels presided over jointly by Shakespeare, Homer and Tolstoy – can draw up a book contract for an author to sign, so scrupulously and tightly drafted that it binds him inescapably to produce, under the most fearsome penalties, a book of the required subject and the required length at the required time; they can make sure that he will not dare to spend the advance on fast women and slow horses; they can insist that they monitor his progress chapter by chapter; they can demand that he provides photographs, diagrams and an index at his own expense; they can leave him in no doubt that if the book results in a libel action they will hold him responsible for all damages and costs; but in this world, and I suspect in the next also, no enforceable contract can contain, even as a sub-clause of a sub-section of a sub-heading, any guarantee that the book, when delivered, will be found to be a masterpiece.

One view holds that unless writers are given more of other people's money literature will die out; the other states that unless writers are given less of other people's noise the same unhappy fate will befall the art. The proponents of the first view cannot accept that the quality of the writing should be the test for a handout ('The contraction in the number of bursaries – on the ground that too much indifferent work had been supported – may have been a tactical mistake'); the advocates of the second welcome the suspicion that the self-publicising shrewdness of the Booker Prize donors has backfired ('the sole beneficiaries of their generosity (are) a handful of rapacious publishers and their lucky authors').

I do not believe that any true work of literature will come out of any scheme of public grants to authors, which would otherwise never have been written; nor do I believe that any scheme of private prizes to unworthy recipients will inhibit any worthy but disappointed writer from producing a true work of literature if that is what he has in him. The often-made analogy with opera and drama is false; for the performance arts hundreds of people are required, with complex relationships and valuable time, and in modern conditions these often cannot be provided at unsubsidised cost. But for a book, all that is required is one man or one woman, equipped with one pencil and one packet of paper.

That simple combination will not be irreparably broken by the sound and fury of the literary circus, nor will it be in the least affected by the production of non-books by non-authors. Neither Harold Robbins nor Marghanita Laski, neither 'the books business' nor the 'lofty elitists', have any power to harm or to create literature, which has never been, cannot be, and never will be, created by anything but the interaction of a single mind and a single soul.

'What is art', asked Samuel Butler, 'that it should have a sake?' We might well ask, and it is not nearly so easy to find an answer as it should be. I rely instead on the Sieve of History. Chatterton died of poverty, but his work lives; Marie Corelli died of diamonds, but hers does not. On the other hand, Thomas Mann was a genius and made a lot of money from his books; the ninety-fifth imitation of *The Day of the Jackal* was neither better nor worse than the original, and was remaindered a fortnight after publication. I tell you that justice does rule the world, and books are not exempt from its judgements, eccentric or capricious though these sometimes seem.

I do not object to the giving of modest sums, provided out of our taxes, to authors considered fitted to receive them. Nor do I object to the giving of huge sums, provided by commercial sponsors, to authors plainly unfitted to receive anything but cries of derision. But the cause of literature will be neither advanced nor set back by either. Mr Booker and Mr de Jongh will stay in after school and write out one hundred times: 'Shakespeare said "Not marble, nor the gilded monuments Of princes, shall outlive this powerful rhyme", and Shakespeare was right.'

The Times November 15th, 1983

A Ring for all seasons

At about seven o'clock in the evening on Monday of last week, in the middle of Act II of *Die Walküre,* Hildegarde Behrens embarked upon the long dialogue in which she brings the tidings of death to the doomed hero, with the words 'Siegmund, sieh auf mich' ('Siegmund, look on me'). At that moment, a puff of white smoke was seen to emerge from the *Festspielhaus* chimney, and the vast throng on the terrace, many of whom had been there, patiently awaiting this moment, for anything up to thirty years, fell to their knees; some were openly weeping, and a few of the more elderly ones, mostly French, expired on the spot, their faces wreathed in beatific smiles. Then the Cardinal-Secretary, Herr Wolfgang Wagner, stepped on to the balcony over the main entrance, gave the traditional blessing, *Urbe et orbi*, and pronounced the fateful words, so long unheard in these parts: 'Habemus Brünnhildam.'

All we need now is a Wotan and a Siegfried, and we shall have the fixings of an uncommonly fine *Ring*.

I paused in Salzburg for a few days en route, to lay in some Mozart, like a man hastily putting on a thick pullover when the pilot announces that all the engines have failed and the aircraft is going to ditch in the sea. I was greeted, alas, by a sign that the world is coming to an end even more rapidly than I had supposed; a McDonald's in the Getreidegasse, almost bang opposite the front door of the Goldener Hirsch. No matter; there was also a *Così Fan Tutte*, lovingly and lingeringly conducted by Muti, with Bruscantini as Alfonso and the finest

Mozart tenor singing I have ever heard in my life, from Francesco Araiza. Then I donned my sandals and my habit of coarse woollen cloth roughly tied with string, put a crust of bread and a few radishes in my scrip, took my staff in hand, and set off on my quinquennial pilgrimage to the holy place of Wagner, to sit in terrible darkness for sixteen hours and there experience once more the effect of this unique music-drama, which bites its victims more deeply than any other work of art I know, and bites them, moreover, with teeth coated in a strange hallucinatory drug which induces a condition well described by the Ancient in Shaw's *Back to Methusaleh:* 'Infant! one moment of the ecstasy of life as we live it would strike you dead.'

Why do we do it? Certainly not to enjoy the delights of Bayreuth, a notoriously undelightful town. (It, too, has a McDonald's, but here it is hardly out of place, for there has been a Parsifal Chemist's in the High Street for at least a quarter of a century, and what I paid for a cummerbund would have kept Wagner in quilted silk dressing-gowns for at least twice as long.) All sensible folk shun Bayreuth entirely, and stay out at Pegnitz with the good Herr Pflaum, whose hotel, now a member of the Relais et Châteaux confraternity, is better run and more comfortable than ever (I have an apartment so enormous that in addition to an ordinary bathroom it sports a jacuzzi pool in solid onyx that takes me ten minutes to wade across), with Brother Hermann in the kitchen muttering spells, to good effect, over the *zicklein knusprig gebraten,* and a young waitress the living image of Maggie Smith.

Why do we do it? Whatever the answer, we are in good company. From where I stand, waiting for the fanfare to summon us back to our seats and wondering whether I have time for another brace of sausages before the interval ends, I can see, among the British contingent alone, a former Prime Minister, a Secretary to the Cabinet, a former Minister of the

Arts, a former chairman of Covent Garden, a royal duke, a Warden of Wadham, a genius, a saviour of Venice, a young composer on his honeymoon, a young barrister on hers (the same one, actually), a director-general, and a man who claims to have acquired a ticket for *Götterdämmerung* this very morning by mingling with the seething crowd outside the box office (sold out since last November) in search of what he called 'the most obviously criminal face I could spot' and, when he spotted it, asking it out of the corner of his mouth whether it had one of the precious pieces of cardboard to sell at double the official price, being instantly rewarded for both his ingenuity and his perspicacity by discovering that he had hit, first go, upon the leading ticket-tout of the Bayreuth Festival, if not of all Bavaria.

But why do we do it? This year, at any rate, there is an extra answer. When Georg Solti and Peter Hall (they are known as *'die Sirs'* in the town) were engaged for the new Bayreuth *Ring,* they promised that they, together with Hall's chosen designer, William Dudley, would give Wagner everything he asked for in the stage directions – settings, supernumeraries and all. ('Even a bear?' I asked Sir Peter incredulously when I heard of this rash promise. 'Even a bear,' he replied with hardly a tremor in his voice. And there it is, in Act I of *Siegfried,* large, brown and furry, and plainly longing to growl.) Now a naturalistic *Ring* has been long overdue; I have not seen the door of Hunding's parlour fly open to admit the moonlight since the late 1940s, and I doubt if Fricka's chariot has been drawn by rams since Wagner died. Well, in this *Ring* the door flies open and the moonlight floods the stage as it floods the orchestra, and when Fricka arrives in the next act she arrives, as Wagner specifies, in a chariot drawn by rams, and very handsome black rams they are, too.

That is by no means all. The forest scenes are beautifully set and staged, their trees like the real trees I see on my way in to Bayreuth on board Herr

Pflaum's festival bus, and the sunlight, falling through their branches, perfectly convincing, as are most of the interiors – Mime's smithy, for instance, and Nibelheim, where Alberich has built himself a golden throne. There is a real rope for the Norns, too, real water for the Rhinemaidens (stark naked, incidentally, though one of them needs to take her bottom to the sunshine on some secluded beach, for at present it is disconcertingly paler than the rest of her) and a truly savage dragon, looking like a cross between a Siberian mammoth and a science-fiction giant lobster. I swear that there are even real flames on the stage for the Immolation, in which case some of the Gibichungs milling around the pyre had better be firemen in disguise.

Nor is it just a matter of authentic props and scene-paintings; the movement, especially for the Rhine-maidens and the Vassals, is as good as anything I have ever seen on the operatic stage, and the great set-pieces – notably the Entry into Valhalla and the Funeral March. –

are replete with imagination and integrity, as indeed are many of the details, such as the dinosaur into which Alberich turns himself in the first transformation instead of the usual snake or dragon (inevitably upstaged later by the real dragon), and the murder of Fasolt by his brother, accomplished not with a club but with a chunk of the fatal gold. The acting, it is true, is mostly no more than a sketch so far, and in some cases hardly even that, but the obvious intentions behind the sketch offer hope for a finished picture next year or the year after.

There are mistakes, of course, the worst of them being Hall's decision to use a gauze, which fuzzes everything, particularly that which should not be fuzzed. Then again, the Valkyries' collection of the bodies from the battlefield is a mess, and the Gibichung Hall, until the final scene, is horribly cramped, besides being carpeted, apparently, in bird-droppings.

Yet a *Ring* cannot be made out of

authenticity alone. Peter Hall's success lies in the way he has enabled us, by his fidelity to the wishes of a composer with a well-deserved reputation for knowing his own mind, to see both the drama and its meanings plain. Away with the 'interpretations' we have had these last years, mostly by salon-Marxists who have never read more than two paragraphs of Marx and understood neither. Away with the incessant hunger to *épater les bourgeois*, to draw parallels that are not parallel and conclusions that conclude nothing. Away with everything that blocks out path into the heart of Wagner's mystery with signposts that claim to be directing us there.

Wagner's great tale of will and power, of love, renunciation and redemption, of sacrifice and self-sacrifice, will speak clearly enough to an audience when the director has the courage – as Hall has had – to let it do so, to seek the truth in the relationships, in the characters and their natures, in the symbolism, in the struggle of strength that cannot be waged through force ('Nichts durch Gewalt!'), in the Shakespearian understanding of the human heart that runs right through this most heroic of dramas. (No director who does not comprehend Shakespeare can succeed in the *Ring,* and Hall is one of our finest Shakespearian directors). The clue lies in the pattern of the *leitmotifs;* these will always guide us to the meanings, great and small, and it is a measure of Hall's success that I cannot remember having seen or heard a *Ring* in which they made Wagner's points, with all their complexity and many sidedness, in a manner at once so urgent, so clear and so illuminating.

But why, I ask yet again, do we do it? Why do we put up with the discomfort, the expense, the monomania all round us, the frightful drivel in the programme-book (this year's coveted Gibberish Prize was won effortlessly by Claude Lévi-Strauss – how did that man acquire a reputation even in our gullible age?), the monstrous demands made upon our time and attention?

We do it for the music, on which we are drunk, hopelessly drunk, from the first intimation of the Rhine as the E flat steals out into the darkness to the final moment, a week later, as the Redemption theme spreads its healing wings in benediction over a world made anew by love.

So far I have concentrated on Peter Hall's direction and William Dudley's settings. Now I must hail Solti's triumph in the pit. (A pit indeed; during the *Siegfried* of the first cycle, the temperature beneath the wooden shell that covers the orchestra touched 111 degrees). Disaster is inevitable in all productions of Wagner; there is no such thing as an understudy, because if you can re-member some of the words and sing most of the notes in more or less the right key you can write your own contract any-where in the world, and this production was horribly beset. From the new Siegfried, Rainer Goldberg, much was expected; he was said to have the true *Heldentenor* voice, and had been preparing for his ordeal for nearly three years. Alas, at the final, public, dress rehearsal he went to pieces, and had to be replaced by Manfred Jung. The trouble with Jung is the same as the trouble with Siegmund Nimsgern, the chosen Wotan; we know the furthest inch of which they are capable, and there was no chance that either would astound us, as Hildegarde Behrens did with her Brünnhilde. So the search continues for the two other legs of the tripod on which every *Ring* must stand, and it is a measure of the plight in which Wagner conductors live that among the names being bandied about for Siegfried was Placido Domingo; why, if I had offered to sing the part myself I could have found a dozen people willing to put me on their list before the end of the interval.

In addition to Behrens, who sang with an amplitude and beauty of tone that made it difficult to believe that this was her first *Ring,* there were only two really outstanding voices: Aage Haugland as Hagen and Jeannine Altmeyer as

Sieglinde, *proxime accessit* for a future Brünnhilde herself. Not enough; all now rested on Solti's shoulders.

His reading was fast (at the end of Act I of *Götterdämmerung* I thought my watch must have stopped, for he took only one hour and fifty minutes, which may be a record), yet although it was full of intensity and force it never seemed hurried, so perfectly paced was it. The spring of nervous energy in Solti's Wagner is now completely flexible, a servant not a master, and the consequence is that it is impossible to imagine better conducting in the *Ring* than he has given us here, or for that matter better playing than he succeeded in drawing from the invisible orchestra.

The climaxes surged forth in all their splendour – the end of *Rheingold,* the *Ride,* the *Götterdämmerung* chorus, Waltraute's flight to her lost sister, the duel, the forging of the sword, the murder of Siegfried – but they never seemed, as they so often do, like separate bits of washing on a line; the great span of Solti's conception held everything in place, everything balanced, everything organic. And he knew when to slow down; the invocation to the unborn hero as Wotan leaves the fire was echoed by the trombones with majestic deliberation, and 'Ruhe, Ruhe, du Gott' was like the placing in position of the final stone of a tomb.

It is impossible, I know, to convince anyone who does not love Wagner's music that it is lovable; either you feel that when you hear it, or it is not for you. I travelled to Salzburg with my friend Count Alois von Vorsicht-Stufe, for instance; the Count is a passionate and profoundly knowledgeable Mozartian, but he declined all suggestions that he should come on to Bayreuth with me. To change his mind, I played him a bit on the way; he listened attentively for about a quarter of an hour, then said in measured tones, 'It's all very interesting, but when does the music start?' It is useless to talk, in these circumstances, of the unbroken thread of melody, of the orchestra as the chief voice, of the way in which the themes are continuously transformed; we know what secret it is that the others do not share. I told the Count, when he begged me to explain to him just what it was that I got out of Wagner, that it was as though every bit of my mind, my body, my psyche and my soul had been unscrewed, sand-blasted, polished for thirty six hours, bathed in the most expensive *eau de cologne,* put together again and gift-wrapped, knowing all the while that those who have not experienced it will not understand, and those who have experienced it will not need to understand. And very rarely indeed have I felt the experience as I just have in Bayreuth.

The greatest coup was in the final bars of *Die Walküre.* For Act III, Hall and Dudley had reverted to the tilting platform that has unfortunately become standard for productions of the *Ring* in recent years. (The Valkyrie sisters had to be anchored when it swung vertically, and Brünnhilde, poor girl, was at one point strapped upside-down beneath it, waiting – for two and a half minutes – until it turned right over and allowed her to get her circulation back). When the platform first appeared, a groan of protest seemed in order, but it was stifled on my lips, and indeed I was unable to make a sound of any kind, by what happened just before the curtain fell.

Wotan has laid his beloved, erring daughter to rest, and summoned Loge to guard her with fire. The ring of red is unbroken around her, and the flames that dim night's candles in the velvet darkness above her are depicted in the music, barring the way to all but the fearless hero who is to awaken her. Wotan, with infinite, resigned pity and regret, strides out of the magic circle and out of the scene. And at the moment the whole platform, with the sleeping heroine clad in her finery of fire, took off like some great space-ship, and went sailing up the sky so that she might sleep, fittingly, among the stars. I knew then the quality of this *Ring* for all seasons, and I knew also exactly why we who love the work do so.

The Times August 16-17th, 1983

De mortuis

The Reverend Oscar Muspratt is the Vicar of Penn, and I must say I rather like the cut of his jib. It was to him that, at the end of last week, there fell the task of conducting the funeral service for Donald Maclean, whose parents are buried in Penn churchyard, and whose son had brought back his ashes from Moscow to lie with them in the family grave; the only other mourners were Maclean's brother and sister-in-law.

Because of the delay caused by traffic conditions, darkness had fallen by the time the burial party was assembled, and the service was conducted by the light of torches held by the vicar and the verger:

> We buried him darkly at dead of
>   night,
> The sods with our bayonets turning
> By the struggling moonbeam's
>   misty light
> And the lanthorn dimly burning.

Mr Muspratt was at pains to defend his decision to allow the traitor's remains a resting-place and to conduct the service, saying that he was expecting criticism for doing so. I dare say he will get it, too, though some of it may come from an unexpected quarter; there are folk whose only complaint will be that Mr Muspratt did not read the Funeral Oration of Pericles at the graveside and laud Maclean as a noble hero who did his bit to bring the delights of Soviet Communism to his native country.

Never mind: the good shepherd did his duty by the blackest of his flock, and explained his action in eloquent terms: 'I thought it through,' he said, 'and decided what was fair and what was right. I can't say I will bury the goodies and toss out the baddies.'

> Lightly they'll talk of the spirit
>   that's gone.
> And o'er his cold ashes upbraid
>   him –
> But little he'll reck, if they let him
>   sleep on
> In the grave where a Briton has laid
>   him.

'A vicar conducting a burial service,' went on Mr Muspratt, 'commends everyone to the mercy of God,' and he will no doubt be cheered to know that I commend his sound grasp of theology. It may be said that Maclean escaped earthly punishment for his earthly wickedness (though I for one do not believe he did – beside a quarter of a century of disillusion in Moscow the flames of hell themselves would seem positively inviting, let alone a stretch in Parkhurst) and that he is therefore all the less worthy of Christian burial. But the

Book of Common Prayer makes no such distinctions; the office for the burial of the dead says that 'We meekly beseech thee, O Father, to raise us from the death of sin unto the life of righteousness,' and goes on to ask that 'at the general Resurrection in the last day, we may be found acceptable in thy sight.' This is all pretty tentative, and could hardly be otherwise without the most appalling presumption, but the hope there expressed is at the heart of the Christian religion; surely even the greatest sinner may be allowed to hope, and even if he does not, a priest may be allowed at his graveside to hope on his behalf – indeed, that is the very office and function of a priest. Besides, as Mr Muspratt said, 'The dead are dead; one has to serve and minister to the living.'

> We thought, as we hollow'd his
>   narrow bed
> And smooth'd down his lonely
>   pillow,
> That the foe and the stranger would

tread o'er his head,
And we far away on the billow!

It is the modern fashion to affect a lack
of interest in the ceremonies that follow
death, and even in the mystery of what
may follow the ceremonies. So much the
worse for the modern fashion, for the
mystery remains one of the most
tremendous questions in the universe,
and the ceremonies, in all ages and
cultures except and until our own, have
been designed to bring home that
tremendousness. The Christian is in-
structed not to question the purpose of
God, which cannot be understood in
earthly terms, but the reward for this
abstinence is the promise of redemption,
which is held out to saint and sinner
alike, and neither sainthood nor sinner-
dom can be guaranteed to turn the scale
in either direction. Heinrich Heine died
with one of history's most splendid jests
on his lips – *'Dieu me pardonnera, c'est son
métier'* – but though Heine was an even
odder Christian than he was a Jew, he

had got a great truth by the tail.

Donald Maclean committed one of the most terrible of crimes, perhaps the most terrible of all, and let us have no more nonsense about misplaced idealism; he did great evil that greater evil might come. Yesterday I stood beside the grave of Rebecca West, one of the noblest spirits I have ever been fortunate to count as a friend; it was from her, moreover, that I learned exactly why treason, like murder, strikes not only at the state and its citizens but at the very fabric of the universe. She would not have gone to Donald Maclean's funeral, and neither would I, but though the Vicar of Penn would certainly share our earthly view of the traitor and his treason, the clerk had business in the churchyard that the laity had not.

It must be said that the worms take much the same view of these matters as Christianity does, and will munch their way as happily through the remains of the dishonourable son as through those of his honourable parents. It is possible, is it not, that the worms and the Christians have, by different routes and with different motives, both come to the right conclusion? We have it on very good authority that, although five sparrows are sold for two farthings, not one of them is forgotten before God; it is not necessary to see what larger purpose Donald Maclean served, provided we can grasp the strange thought that such purpose might have existed. The sparrows, it is true, did not betray their country, but I doubt if God is quite so literal; I am not a Christian, but I do not find it *very* difficult to believe that there is a category in which, just as there shall be neither Greek nor Jew, circumcision nor uncircumcision, Barbarian, Scythian, bond nor free, so the line between loyal and disloyal shall be likewise erased.

That category is not to be found on earth. But the Vicar of Penn's charity was not of the earthly kind, and anyway we do not even know, you and I and the vicar, what remorse gnawed at Maclean through the solitary years, let alone *in articulo mortis.* If he had returned to Britain and stood trial, he would have been rightly condemned and rightly punished. If another judgment, whether harsher or less harsh than the judgement of men, awaited him in that country churchyard, it was outside our understanding, and the vicar was right to insist, in the absence of clear evidence to the contrary, that it hath pleased Almighty God to take unto himself the soul of our dear brother here departed. To bury a man in consecrated ground is to say nothing about him other than that God may have a use for his soul, and what Christian priest could say less? There are still plenty, after all, to render unto Caesar the things that are Caesar's:

Few and short were the prayers we
    said,
And we spoke not a word of sorrow;
But we steadfastly gazed on the face
    that was dead,
And we bitterly thought of the
    morrow.

The Times March 22nd, 1983

Origins and lemmings

The other day I wrote a column about the tireless efforts being made by some liberals to ruin their own party. The head-line was 'For Liberals read lemmings'.

Whenever a newspaper article figures in legal proceedings – in a libel action, say – somebody has to explain to the judge and the lawyers that writing journalists do not write their own head-lines. This is partly for technical reasons with which I shall not burden you, and partly because the art of headline-writing is not at all the same as the art of writing the words underneath; many of the most gifted of newspaper journalists do not have that particular skill at all.

Headlines are written by people called sub-editors, and it was they who wrote the headline I have referred to. The subs, as we call them, are an odd but endearing species; no one who has seen them emerging, at edition time, from nearby burrows (called 'pubs'), blinking at the light and licking the last drops off their whiskers, can fail to warm to the merry creatures, in appearance somewhat resembling koala-bears and really not unlike lemmings themselves. All sensible journalists take care to make friends of the subs; my own relations with them, I am happy to say, are of the most cordial, and not only because I always have a biscuit or two or a knob of sugar in my pockets when I go to see them.

The headline, likening Liberals to lemmings, was inspired, obviously, by the strange habit that lemmings have, well documented through the years, of rushing down to the sea in enormous numbers and drowning themselves.

There are two principal theories to explain this curious behaviour. The more romantic is the belief that the lemmings have a deeply rooted biological memory of a sunken continent which, millions of years ago, they inhabited, and that their mass suicides are the fruits of a desperate attempt to find again their lost home or perish in the attempt.

This well-supported and strongly held belief was enshrined in verse by a former poet laureate, John Masefield:

Once in a hundred years the
    Lemmings come
Westward, in search of food, over
    the snow;
Westward, until the salt sea drowns
    them dumb;
Westward, till all are drowned,
    those Lemmings go.
Once, it is thought, there was a
westward land (Now drowned)
where there was food for those
    starved things,
And memory of the place has

119

burnt its brand
In the little brains of all the
Lemmings kings. . .

The less haunting but more widely
held theory for the lemmings' periodic
mass suicides, one which fits better into
our gloomy times, is that they do it
deliberately, out of an excess of
Weltschmerz, and it is this explanation that
has made the lemming so popular a
metaphor for those who wish to point to
heedless self-destructive urges among
humankind; there must by now be
several hundred thousand printed refer-
ences to the 'lemming-like' behaviour of
the nuclear powers in their arms race.

Masefield touches upon the second
version, too, and its human analogue, for
the rest of the poem I have quoted runs
as follows:

Perhaps, long since, there was a
land beyond
Westward from death, some city,
some calm place

Where one could taste God's quiet
    and be fond
With the little beauty of a human
    face;
But now the land is drowned. Yet
    still we press
Westward, in search, to death, to
    nothingness.

Now scientists will have none of these theories; lemmings drown themselves in huge numbers, but the experts, though they cannot explain the phenomenon, reject both the belief that the lemmings behave thus in search of Atlantis and the conjecture that they do so to fill *Daily Telegraph* leading articles. Another Poet Laureate, Robert Bridges, was of this more hard-headed school, saying in *The Testament of Beauty* (I am sorry about his horrible orthography) that:

Ther is no tradition among the
lemmings of Norway how their
progenitors, when their offspring
    increased,

bravely forsook their crowded nestes
in the snow, swarming upon the
plains to ravage field and farm, and
in unswerving course ate their way
to the coast, where plunging down
the rocks they swam in the salt
  sea
to drowning death; nor hav they in
acting thus today any plan for their
journey or prospect in the event.

All the foregoing sets out simply the
reasons for the place the lemming holds
in the imagination of millions who have
never set eyes on one of them; whence the
headline on my column. What now follows should not be read by those with a
history of heart trouble, for the shock to
the nervous system that my readers are
about to experience might well prove too
much for the particularly susceptible.

Lemmings don't. They don't, that is, rush
down to the sea and drown themselves,
whether in search of a sunken land, or
because they have run out of Nembutal,
or for any other reason. They do take

part in gigantic migrationary move-ments, and there is evidence that these follow a cyclical pattern – not once a century, as Masefield says, but probably every four years; the reason for these mass uprootings is still not clear, though it seems to have something to do with po-pulation pressure. In the course of the migrations, with hordes of lemmings simultaneously on the march, some inevitably get drowned in streams and fjords, and when they reach the coasts many drown in the attempt to reach offshore islands. But the Gadarene Lemming is a mythical animal, and the real one – *Lemmus lemmus* – is entitled to complain about many decades of de-famation.

The greatest scholar of lemming-lore is Dr Charles Elton, sometime director of the Bureau of Animal Population in Oxford, his book on the subject, *Voles, Mice and Lemmings* (OUP, 1942), which disposes of many lemming myths, in-cluding the one which holds that they are rained from the clouds, is still the standard work on subject, though there is an excellent, more popular work by Walter Marsden, called *The Lemming Year* (Chatto, 1964) and of course no serious student of the subject can ignore Wildhagen's *Om vekslingene i bestandan av smagnagere i Norge*.

All leading authorities, however, and all field studies, are adamant that the verdict of *felo de se* is, and always has been, a miscarriage of justice; Elton says that 'When a lemming cannot avoid meeting a man he will often sit on his hind legs and hop up and down as if in excited anger and charge the intruder, who may get his hand bitten deeply if he tries to pick the animal up,' and it seems very likely that the lemming's anger and aggressive behaviour have been excited by the tenancious but unjust belief in its suicidal tendencies.

Though the lemming has figured in folklore for a good many centuries, the mass drowning belief is, interestingly enough, a twentieth-century creation. It is, I suppose, a sophisticate's myth, appealing in its deliberate-suicide aspect to fashionable modern pessimism and in its Atlantis-search form to the equally fashionable yearning for a new, pure world elsewhere. Professor Bergen Evans, in that most entertaining work *The Natural History of Nonsense (Michael Joseph, 1947)*, points out that it is a popular belief with the *New Yorker*, but the role of lemming mythopoeist to the gentry must long since have been taken over by the *New York Review of Books*.

I do not suppose that my words today will kill the lemming legend; I have often pointed out in vain that Canute did not suppose he could make the waves turn back (he commanded them to do so in order to show up his courtiers, who insisted that he had such powers, for the fools they were), and I have also fruitlessly explained that Cloud-cuckoo-land, invariably used as an insult, is in fact a high compliment, for in Aristophanes' play *The Birds,* Nephelococcugia, or Cloud-cuckoo-land, the kingdom established by the birds midway between heaven and earth, triumphantly brings both gods and men to subjection. Myths, however, have their own power – they would not be myths if they did not – and I do not expect the suicidal lemming to vanish from the earth after today. Still, it might vanish from a few newspaper headlines; and with even that much of an achievement I would be well content.

The Times September 6th, 1983

Murder most fashionable

A *Daily Express* gossip-columnist the other day quoted some remarks made by Claus von Bulow, the Danish-born American who was convicted earlier this year of trying to murder his wife by injecting her with powerful doses of insulin. (She did not die, but lapsed into a coma, apparently irreversible; at any rate she has not regained consciousness after more than six months.) Von Bulow, who is out on bail pending appeal, continues to protest his innocence, and we should remember that that is something done by innocent men as well as guilty ones; in any case, I have nothing to say about the outcome of the trial, let alone of the appeal.

What I *have* something to say about is his claim that most of his friends and many strangers have offered him sympathetic encouragement. He puts forward this information to strengthen his insistence that he is innocent, and in the course of doing so makes the statement that caught my imagination. 'The crime I am said to have committed', he says, 'was unspeakable, and if people believed I had done it they would not treat me in this way.'

Unfortunately – for us rather than him – the apparently logical conclusion is based on a false premise: our world is littered with people who would not think it at all odd to stop a man in the street and offer him their support (which is what von Bulow says is constantly happening to him) though they thought him guilty of an unspeakable attempt at murder.

Not long before the von Bulow case there was the matter of Jack Henry

Abbott, who was made almost as famous and popular by Norman Mailer as the murderers of *In Cold Blood* had been by Truman Capote. Abbott was – is – a murderer who began to write to Mr Mailer from prison; he is clearly a man who knows a sucker when he sees one. His letters describe horrible conditions and treatment in the prisons he has been in; some of it, even much of it, may well be true, though confidence in his veracity is not strengthened (except, no doubt, in the mind of Mr Mailer) by passages like this:

> The judge sentenced me to the main penitentiary for the express purpose of having me raped by prisoners and reduced to a homosexual . . . To the authorities, there is nothing seriously wrong with anyone getting raped in prison. On the contrary, the idea excites them; they *enjoy* it.

Anyway, Mr Mailer got together a group of like-minded savants, and with a long pull, a strong pull and a pull all together they managed to obtain parole for Abbott, an event celebrated by a fashionable dinner-party *chez* Mailer. Unfortunately, the guest of honour, pausing only to put his letters to his benefactor into a handy volume (published in this country by Hutchinson) and to knock off an article or two for the *New York Review of Books,* promptly committed another murder – of, it is worth noting, an unprovoked and particularly brutal kind – and was returned to the hoosegow, leaving Mr Mailer in a state of pained bewilderment and the victim of Mr Mailer's friend in a state of rapidly advancing de-composition.

Let us not take a too elevated cis-atlantic view of these events. The Kray twins graced many a modish London gathering in their murderous heyday, and when Charles Richardson wrote his famous letter to *The Times* I am sure that the people who concluded from it that he was a much misunderstood man greatly outnumbered those who felt that he had provided the best reason yet devised for abolishing the Open University.

Nor should we forget George Davis; he didn't murder anybody, but about a quarter of an hour after getting out of prison as a result of a campaign in this country similar to the Abbott boom in the United States (you can still see 'George Davis is innocent' painted on walls in London) he was tastelessly photographed by some brash *paparazzo* (apparently indifferent to the Press Council's severe condemnation of 'snatched' pictures) in the very act of holding up a bank with a sawn-off shotgun.

There is a phrase – I think it is Alexander Woollcott's – about 'a girlish enthusiasm for mere biceps', and there is something of that at work here. Not long ago it was fashionable for the daughters of the peerage to form liaisons on the far side of Aldgate Pump with some of the more cauliflower-eared practitioners of gbh, and the excitement generated by the combination of violence and armpits that attracted the Hon. Sophonisba was not entirely confined to her own sex (quite apart from the homosexual *demi-monde* that overlapped with the world of the Krays).

But the deliciously guilty thrill that some obtain from contemplating, at a safe distance, a criminal brutality is inadequate to explain those who want to shake the hand of Claus von Bulow, not because they think he is innocent but because they think he is guilty, or those who clinked glasses with Jack Henry Abbott and so thoroughly encouraged him to dwell in his fantasies that they were subsequently obliged to feel quite mortified when he went a little too far, or those who indignantly agreed with Charles Richardson when he argued that it was society's fault, not his, that he was a ruthless and sadistic gangster.

Once upon a time, it was smart to wear certain clothes, to eat at certain restaurants, to take holidays at certain expensive resorts. Now palates having grown jaded, smartness comes in sharper flavours; it is smart to sniff cocaine, to watch pornographic videotapes, to despise the clumsy processes of democratic government, above all to affect a moral relativism that puts a murderer's qualities as an entertaining dinner-guest above his qualities as a murderer.

For this new smart set life is either literature or a series of sociological experiments, and is in any case without responsibility; when there is no one to answer to, there is nothing to answer. Claus von Bulow may or may not have tried to murder his wife in a particularly vile manner, and in doing so reduced her existence to that of a vegetable, but the parties he gave before this misfortune fell upon him were among Newport's finest, so let us cross the road and shake his hand. Jack Henry Abbott may have stuck a knife into a waiter whose manner had displeased him, and then twisted the knife round in his dying body, but Mr Norman Mailer, who 'can afford the sophisticated despair of finding Russia altogether as abominable as America', says that Abbott may be 'a new writer of the largest stature', and there are few judges of new writers, or for that matter of the size of statures, to compare with Mr Mailer. Charles Richardson may have watched, laughing, as his victims suffered, but anyone can see that was the fault of the social *mores* of his *milieu*. If you will forgive me for quoting myself, I shall repeat what I wrote at the time of the Blunt affair. 'There are those who live by an enervated reason that owns no master in the soul, and who can find arguments that enable them to claim that the atrophy of the moral sense from which they suffer is in fact a form of rational judgement.'

The trouble with people who hobnob with fashionable murderers – and indeed choose which murderers are to *be* fashionable and then make them so – is that if they were asked not *whether* it is wrong to do murder, but *why* it is wrong, they would be unable to say, and for the most part would quite literally be unable to see any meaning at all in the question. But if we do not know why murder is wrong then we are as dead as the victim of the least fashionable murderer; even Raskolnikov, in the end, came to know the answer.

It is possible to believe that Claus von Bulow was wrongly convicted. But if you do not believe that, it is impossible for you to shake his hand in merry friendship and save your soul alive. You say you haven't got a soul to save? I rest my case.

The Times November 15th, 1982

Beyond the fringe

It is a truth not sufficiently appreciated that any political proposal which commends itself to both front benches of the House of Commons is at best useless and at worst against the public interest; one which also appeals to both main parties' back benches is likely to be a constitutional outrage and certain to be seriously damaging to the people's liberty, prosperity or both.

Such is the proposed Representation of the People Bill, of which it can be safely said that the matter of improving the people's representation never so much as entered the heads of the Conservative and

Labour politicians who took part in the discussions that led to the Government's White Paper, their sole concern being to reinforce and extend their monopoly of power, or, to put it in plain English, to get more of their bread into more of our gravy; it's God's mercy that they didn't include a provision to double their own salaries and link their pensions to an automatic annual increase of four times the rate of inflation, and they will probably try to shove that bit in on the Report stage if we don't watch out, or even if we do.

In case there is any monoglot Kalmuck newly arrived among us this morning who does not understand what I am talking about, I had better make clear that it is not the extension of the franchise to those on holiday; what makes me think more kindly of Guy Fawkes, Oliver Cromwell and the German pilot who scored a direct hit on the House of Commons during the Blitz is the proposed intention to raise the electoral deposit to a thousand pounds. (The original plan had been to make it *two* thousand pounds, but they magnanimously changed their minds in the course of the discussions).

The arguments with which this shameful measure has been supported are impudent even beyond the calls of self-interest. First, it is said that when the deposit was instituted (in 1918) the value of money was much greater, so that in equivalent terms £150 should today, be even more than £1,000. Oh yes? And what pray, was the standard percentage of income-tax at that time? And what were average rates? And where was VAT? And how many more of the imposts, mulctings, duties, levies, tariffs, licences, exactions, fees, dues, tolls, assessments, excises, *gabelles* and capitations now laid upon our backs then existed? And how many small parties or unmoneyed Independents were interested in contesting elections then? And when is the cost of a dog-licence going to be raised, in line with the rate of inflation, for the first time since *it* was instituted, in

1878? (When dog-owners cease to have votes, that's when).

Second, it is claimed that the cost of the state of a candidature at a parliamentary election is much higher than £150, so that candidates with no hope of election are being subsidised. So they are; so are the candidates *with* hope of election, and they are quite determined to keep things that way, for the only substantial state-paid election cost that can be attributed to individual candidates is the free mailing to all voters, which every candidate is entitled to claim, and this does not in practice benefit 'fringe' candidates at all, since very few of them can afford the printing of the leaflets which the free postal service would distribute, and even fewer have the manpower to address and fill the envelopes. In other words, the arguments against subsidising candidates does not apply to the new proposal's victims, but it does apply to the instigators; the cost of the free mailing for the Conservative and Labour parties in a general election (reckoning it as second-class post) is roughly £10 million.

Next, it is contended that the proliferation of eccentric candidates tends to bring the election process into disrepute, a charge which, when I first read it, had the unprecedented effect of rendering me incapable of speech for nearly half an hour; beside the Hattersleys and Healeys, the Proctors and Dickenses, Screaming Lord Sutch was a model of dignity and political uprightness, and a bloody sight funnier into the bargain.

But all that is only by way of refutation of the false claims made on behalf of the new Bill. Much more important is the fact that it will damage democracy, which is no doubt why the Home Office is in favour of it, the attitude of the present Home Secretary to democracy being the same as that of a Victorian maiden aunt to masturbation – he has no idea what it is and would not dream of asking, but is convinced that it makes you go blind. Cannot the two main parties lift their eyes for a moment over the rim of the trough and see how important to the vigour and health of our political life is a constant ebb and flow of people and groups who refuse allegiance to the established parties, and how essential it is that such people and groups shall have *full* access to the political system in all its forms, most particularly in its electoral aspect?

If we are going to deny to the Communist Party and the National Front, the SWP and Vanessa's Loonies, the Ecology Party and Commander Bill Boaks, the genuine (as opposed to purely theoretical) right to put up as full a slate of candidates as they wish and can afford, and if we are going to go even further and deny that right to all but a rich handful of the brave and splendid men and women who stand as genuine Independents, unattached even to the smallest and weirdest of the political *groupuscules,* then we might as well deny them free speech as well, together with the right to publish their views and to solicit support for them. (I wouldn't be in the least surprised to learn that a discussion paper enshrining just such proposals is circulating in the Home Office at this very moment).

If economic monopolies, whether of capital or labour, are inimical to economic advance, how much more are political monopolies to political progress! Just imagine a political Britain in which the Conservative and Labour parties have their way and extinguish altogether every rival variety of political appeal, starting with the Alliance, against whom, of course, this measure is chiefly directed. Both parties are at present ossified and bureaucratic to an extent which renders them largely indisting-uishable from whichever prehistoric monster it was that took twenty minutes to register with its brain the fact that a rival had bitten its tail off; give them another inch of exclusive political rights and they will take another dozen miles of arrogance, chicanery and selfishness.

No doubt the Labour Party will assert

that it is not responsible for a government Bill, and – since the contents of it were decided by a Select Committee, not a Speaker's Conference – they are not committed to it. They may even, to keep up a show, attack the clause which gives an absentee vote to those British citizens living abroad. It will all be wool-pulling; this measure is the fruit of a corrupt bargain between Conservatives and Labour, and I do not think the adjective is too strong. All the main provisions of the Bill were agreed by the Select Committee; the fact is that in return for Labour support over the holiday franchise (believed by psephologists to favour the Tories) the Government has offered the lowering of the deposit-losing share of the vote from one-eighth to one-twentieth, thus sparing the Labour Party such hideous and damaging humiliations as their 119 lost deposits of 1983, for under the proposed new rule they would have lost fewer than a dozen. (It is, I may add, particularly dishonest of Labour to sell itself in this fashion, for the original deposit was brought in to limit the chances of the nascent Labour Party, as the present change is designed to hinder the Alliance).

When this matter was discussed, last week, on Sir Robin Day's *Question Time,* before a studio audience, Dr Rhodes Boyson, for the Tories, put forward the argument that the Bill was to be commended because it would discourage 'extremist parties'. It is a measure of the political vanity which grips the two main parties that even a normally merry and realistic fellow like Dr Boyson can thus render himself incapable of noticing that an extremist party, while it remains within the law, has as much right to propogate its doctrines as he has. And that 'incapable of noticing' is the literal truth; so imbued are both main parties with the belief that they are entitled to *all* the political power and patronage and pelf that our system offers them, which is no little, that they have no idea how monstrous, and how dangerous, is their determination to change the law to ensure that not even the smallest challenge to their monopoly may be mounted except on crippling financial terms.

It is worth recording the fact that when Sir Robin put the question to the audience, a great majority – at least two to one – were against the proposal. But implacably opposed as the established politicians are to sharing power with their less official rivals, they are a hundred times more adamant that they will never share it with the people.

The Times February 7th, 1984

Monty Verdi to the rescue

Caliban lives. I deduce this from the goings-on at the Royal Festival Hall and its two adjacent concert-rooms, the Queen Elizabeth Hall and Purcell Room; all three are owned by the GLC, as the heirs of the LCC which built them, and not long ago the rulers of the GLC sacked the manager, and took over the direct running of the halls themselves.

One of the earliest fruits of the change was the scandal of the Soviet propaganda exhibition staged there (at a peppercorn rent); when the details were being worked out, the GLC did not even insist on being allowed to stage a reciprocal exhibition in

Moscow, so eager were they to let Londoners know that the Soviet Union is a peace-loving democracy, brimming over with freedom, prosperity and scrupulous concern for the neighbours. (Mind you, a GLC-sponsored exhibition about us would probably have depicted little but accounts of the oppressed wage-slaves in today's Britain and of their struggle to obtain the vote and the right to form trade unions, with huge oil-paintings by Mr Michael Meacher of the said wage-slaves being batoned by police wearing swastika armbands).

Ever since, the GLC has been resisting, by evasion and delay, any attempts to let Londoners see the other side of the argument, and even now, when they have at last made a half-hearted apology for the Soviet show, they have made it clear that they will not permit any serious or general criticism of the Soviet Union on premises under their control; their only concession is to allow a group working on behalf of Jews who wish to leave the Soviet Union to participate in an Amnesty International exhibition.

At the same time, the new rule at the RFH has brought some substantial improvements – the very attractive liveliness that the foyers now display, largely owing to the outstanding service provided in the buffets by the new caterers, and the improved box office arrangements. (There are the usual rubbishy 'souvenirs' on sale, of course, but even these are more than set off by the excellent bookshop.)

All the same, whatever happens in the surroundings of a concert-hall, good or bad or both, it will and must be judged on what happens inside it. So far, nothing very different has taken place; the GLC have put on various performances and exhibitions in furtherance of their political beliefs (though none, of course, furthering contrary views), but the music remains much the same. As far as I know, there have been no suggestions that bookings will be more readily accepted if the programmes contain more of the works of Alan Bush or loyal contemporary Soviet composers, nor has anybody hinted that putting on performances by Rostropovich, Ashkenazy and other defectors from their glorious Soviet fatherland will be looked on askance. I think I detect a slight tendency to dilute the contents of programmes with a higher proportion of very familiar works, but that, if it is happening, could well be defended (if, indeed, it needs to be defended at all) as sensible commercial practice by the promoters.

Now, however, Caliban has emerged from his lair, blinking at the light and mumbling his watchword: elitist. Mr Peter Pitt, chairthing of the GLC committee under whose auspices the South Bank halls are run, has determined that 'We want more working class and black audiences.' It is a laudable desire, and he is not the first to feel it; the Workers' Educational Association and many similar organisations were conceived in the same spirit. But there is one great, and terrible, difference between the pioneers of art for the masses and the present attitude of the GLC. The former wanted – it was, in many cases, the mainspring of their existence – to illumine the lives of the poor, the uneducated, the despairing, by making sure that they had cheap access to the best that art and craft had created throughout the ages. The wiser among these pioneers knew that those who availed themselves of what was offered would always be a minority, as indeed they have always been a minority among the rich, the educated and the confident; but the pioneers, from William Morris to Arnold Wesker, as they laboured in this field, have always preferred to light candles rather than curse the darkness.

But they never wanted to burn people with the candles. Mr Pitt says 'I don't think many people from my constituency of Hounslow go to the South Bank.' If not, it is a pity, but it is a pity because the musical glories to be found on the South Bank – at, incidentally, ludicrously low prices (£2.80 for the *Missa Solemnis* under

Haitink, £1.50 for Ida Haendel playing the Beethoven Violin Concerto, £2.30 for Bach's *St John Passion*) – would enrich the lives of the people of Hounslow, or even the life of Mr Pitt, just as much as they enrich me.

Mr Pitt is not willing to go out and presuade his constituents to try a spot of Chopin, Mozart and other long-haired intellectuals. No, his approach can be understood from the following statement of his credo: 'There are class and race institutionalised barriers here that need to be broken.' Before a claim as mad and pitiful as that (what West Indian, what labourer, has ever been refused service at the RFH Box Office, or sneered at by the white toffs in the next seat?), Beethoven himself would have been tempted to erase the bit about *Seid umschlungen, Millionen* in the Ninth Symphony. But Mr Pitt's intention, which might well have struck Goering as a bit extreme, is now clear. If the masses will not go to art, so much the worse for art. *Delenda est Carthago.*

Therefore, it is announced, we are to

have wrestling and snooker at the Festival Hall; parallel delights are being devised for the QEH and the Purcell Room. When the four principal symphony orchestras were asked to think of ways to increase South Bank audiences, the management of the Royal Philharmonic suggested bussing in factory workers, and the LPO proposed to add the Festival Hall to the Albert Hall as a venue for its industrial concerts. But such plans were rejected, and soon the grunts and groans of the judo-artists will mingle with the click of the balls on the green baize, in place of the sounds that South Bank audiences since 1951 and indeed audiences all over the world for half a thousand years, have been used to.

Well, well, we must move with the times. But we need not move with them before expressing our opinion of them. The contempt of the far left for the people whose interests they claim to have at heart is notorious. At election-time the workers have been 'brainwashed by the media'; at public libraries they cannot be trusted to reject distasteful attitudes, so books containing these must be censored off the shelves; in their trade unions they might vote the wrong way if they had secret ballots for their officials, so they must not be allowed to have such ballots; in the Festival Hall foyer they might form views unfavourable to the Soviet Union if such views are on offer there, so offer them access to favourable ones only; and upstairs in the auditorium let them be content with the pig-swill that is all they deserve or are capable of enjoying.

Surely this must be the only era in history, other than that of Nazi Germany, in which excellence is not something to admire and strive for, to encourage and to share, but something to hate and mock, to root out and destroy. In education, the whole thrust of the left is to pull down anything that might set standards for emulation. In housing, the local authority that insists that all front doors must be the same colour is driven by the same hunger for uniformity among the masses. In politics, the

growing intolerance on the left –
displayed in the hounding out of Labour
MPs who will not toe the new line and
the shouting down of any opposing voice
at meetings – has reached epidemic
proportions. And in art, anything that
has provided for human beings, and can
still provide, a literally infinite breadth
and depth of beauty, passion, enlightenment, understanding, inspiration and
balm is 'elitist', and must be rejected.

Caliban lives indeed; and he was
always averse to seeing his face in the
mirror. But now he has people to smash
the mirror for him, and the seven years'
bad luck that breaking a mirror entails
will be borne by the rest of us. And paid
for by us, too; the Festival Hall interior
will have to be practically rebuilt for an
evening of wrestling or snooker, all at
prodigious cost. But Caliban now has
unlimited access to our money, and
unlimited willingness to spend it for his
own dark ends. Art on the South Bank,
it seems, may have to go into exile, like
the government of a nation subjugated by

tyranny, until the GLC is swept away and the free republic of true civilisation restored.

The Times February 22nd, 1984

Of tops

We are told on exceptionally good authority that all they that take the sword shall perish with the sword. What is less well known is that all they that take the publicity shall likewise be brought low by the very instrument they have sought to conquer with. The tale which illustrates this truth is one peculiarly of our time; indeed, it could not have taken place in any earlier era. And the moral is not necessarily obvious.

A year or so ago, a young lady among the spectators at a televised rugby international at Twickenham decided, on a sudden impulse, to remove her upper garments and reveal to the cameras and the viewing public that which, or more precisely those which, lay beneath.

What the butler saw, next moment, was an exceptionally substantial bosom, surmounted by an attractive smile. No doubt some of the staider followers of the game (the game of rugby, that is), to whom the turf of Twickers is holy ground, fell down dead at the sight, but for the rest of us (the less expensive Sunday newspapers, next day, featured the lady's development at roughly life-size) the episode served to brighten a chilly weekend, to be pronounced harmless – I forget whether whitehousian moralists declared at the time that the total collapse of civilisation was now inevitable – and to be quickly forgotten.

It was not, however, to be forgotten quite so quickly by the protagonist of the drama, nor was the course of her life destined to continue in quite so pleasant and light-hearted a manner. It seems that today she is without employment, overdrawn at her bank, heavily in debt to the

Inland Revenue, pregnant but unmarried, and living, for want of means, in a friend's house, where she shares a room with her younger sister.

If there were any who denounced the bosom-baring as the kind of thing the Declining Romans got up to in their more imaginative moments, they are no doubt now pursing their lips in great satisfaction and concluding that the wages of sin, if not going as far as death, certainly include insolvency, unmarried motherhood and the condemnation of all right-thinking persons. Take your jumper off at Twickenham and the wrath of God is inevitable; if she'd taken her knickers off as well she would certainly have been struck by lightning ere now.

That is not my view, of course. If it was Providence that punished the lady in that fashion, Providence must have a singularly nasty mind. (Particularly, I may say, since the lady seems to have an exceptionally nice one; she has just said that she feels no resentment for the father of her child, that although he is not himself married 'it would not be right to name him', and that she will not be asking him for money.) But what interests me, and provides my real theme, is not the lady's original action, nor her present misfortunes, but the bit in between.

The immediate consequence of her action was her launching, on a sea of *réclame*, into a many-sided new life (she had been, until the fateful day, an assistant in a bookshop). She made a pop record; she opened a boutique; offers of modelling engagements fell thick and fast upon her doormat.

Note carefully the constituent elements of her new triple career, its nature almost incredibly representative of the froth and bubble that this age mistakes for substance. The characteristic sound of our time and place is the howling and gibbering of pop singers; its characteristic product is the shoddy of the King's Road and Carnaby Street, its characteristic activity is posing, with expressionless faces, for the cameras of advertising photographers. The innocent young lady at Twickenham had noticed, as had the rest of us, these phenomena, and had noticed, again like others, that many of those engaged in such trades had become successful and rich – some of them, indeed, rich almost beyond imagining. Why should she not believe the agents and promoters, the spivs and *tummlers,* who told her that she was no less gifted than the successful ones (which was probably true), and could therefore become no less rich?

You can conjugate it as an irregular verb: I am a pop-singer, you own a boutique, she models, we are successful and rich. Why indeed should not the Lady of Twickenham believe that there is a crock of gold at the end of the rainbow, when in our society a bishop scurries across the country to sit at the feet of Mr Mick Jagger and nod sagely at the pearls of wisdom that fall from his ample lips?

'Everyone seems to think,' she says in recounting her disillusionment, 'that because I'm famous I must be rich.' That ought to be carved on the twentieth century's tombstone, not because the lady has so painfully spotted the fallacy, but because she has so artlessly, yet so truly, defined what today is fame. It is to make records so undemanding of emotion, thought or music that they will get into the 'charts'; it is to sell 'designer jeans' and 'costume jewellery' (if there is any more room on the tombstone those phrases ought to be added), it is to narrow the eyes and point one hip and find the resultant picture amid the glossy trash of the latest giveaway property magazine; for that matter, it is to find the proprietor of the latest giveaway property magazine appointed Rector of the Royal College of Art.

As it chanced, the lady in this case failed to become rich. The boutique did not find favour, the record did not sell millions of copies, the modelling offers did not continue; she now presumably, knows what song the sirens sang. But it might so easily have been otherwise. In our era, some have become millionaires by putting rubbishy records on gramophones; others have made even greater fortunes by gyrating to the records in 'discotheques'; attractive young women have ensured themselves a place in the history books, or at any rate Madame Tussaud's, by looking half-daft for hours on end in a photographic studio. Who will dare say that the young lady of Twickenham was barred from such glories by lack of talent?

And where was the lesson taught that was thus dearly learnt? Who told the disc jockeys and the boutique-owners and the gossip columnists and the disco-dancers and the models that at the end of the rainbow there was gold to be got for the stooping? Why, those who, in the older arts, cottoned on much earlier to the fact that imagination, hard work and the stuff of creation were no longer necessary for success. Do you curl your lip at those who seek fame and fortune through the dubious portals of publicity? Then be prepared to encompass a good deal more in your curl.

For we live in a world that is not exclusively composed of froth; there is the sour lees beneath it to be considered. You can pile bricks for £4,000 a pile if you are in favour at the Tate Gallery; if you tear up the pages of an Act of Parliament and stick them on a wall you may find yourself commended by Mr Richard Cork; if you cover 54 square feet of canvas with rubbish Mr Norman Rosenthal will hang it in the Royal Academy, and if you cover 500 square feet with even greater rubbish Mr Christos Joachimides will hang it in the very next room. Meanwhile, if you are a composer, or want to be thought one, you may write 'works in which the voice has no fixed relation to the score', 'works whose performance is indeterminate' and 'works based on imperfections in the manuscript paper,' and Herr H. H. Stuckenschmidt will write an admiring book about you. Alternatively, you can write poetry by cutting words of newspapers and pasting them together at random; the editors of literary magazines will be eager to publish the results and will squeal like stuck pigs if the Arts Council will not pay them to do so.

It seems hard on the young lady at the rugger match, who did nothing more wicked than believe what she had been told about the value of publicity, that she should now be in want while others, no more talented than she, should have waxed rich as accidentally as she has now waxed poor. Their fame, of course, will last, by history's reckoning, only an instant longer than hers, and she did, after all, cheer us all up, which is more than most of them can say; would the Sunday papers bother to print pictures of Stockhausen's chest, or Carl André's, or Snoo Wilson's?

Good luck, say I, to the lady with the torso that *did* provide pictures, who seems to be a brave lass as well as a good-hearted one; 'I may be down', she says, 'but I'm not out.' I wonder, however, whether she feels that she might have done better to stay at her job in the bookshop and keep all her clothes on. She says herself that she did not earn more than £8,000 from first to last after her moment of fame, and is now £7,000 in debt. But if she were still behind the counter selling the works of Tolstoy, Sophocles and Levin, I calculate that she would have made some £5,400. And what is more, had she remained in the bookshop she might, when trade was slack, have taken down the appropriate volume of Shakespeare and read these words by way of warning:

> All that glisters is not gold;
> Often you have heard that told;
> Many a man his life hath sold
> But my outside to behold;
> Gilded tombs do worms infold.
> Had you been as wise as bold,
> Young in limbs, in judgement old,
> Your answer had not been
>   inscroll'd;
> Fare you well; your suit is cold.

The Times March 20th, 1984

Of bottoms

Today we have naming of parts. A week ago, a nobly-born lady, no less than the sister of the Marquess of Dufferin, and not only of Dufferin but of Ava to boot, was mortally insulted at Greenham Common, where she had gone in order to write an article about the nuclear ladies. The nature of the insult is such that I have hesitated long before deciding to give it wider currency, and readers of a respectable disposition would be well advised to consider very carefully whether they would not do better to stop reading this column immediately; in any case I have to give formal notice that neither I nor the Editor of *The Times* can accept any responsibility for any ill-effects suffered by those who stay with me to what I am obliged to call, with dreadful appositeness in the circumstances I am about to relate, the bitter end.

Lady Caroline Hamilton-Temple-Blackwood, to name but a few, has revealed that in the course of her visit a busload of airmen turned their backs, pulled down their trousers and displayed their buttocks to her, with intent to offend. She has described the scene with a vividness that bodes well for future article about the Greenham protestors, and I cannot do better than repeat her very words. 'They were bending over like ostriches,' she said; 'I had a girl assistant with me and we were both shocked and appalled. I have never seen something so unpleasant.'

I dare say; no wonder she is, according to one report, 'writing to the commander of the camp to demand an explanation', and according to another 'consulting lawyers with a view to bringing a complaint.' (If she does decide to take legal action, I can warmly recommend a barrister with much experience of this kind of thing, Sir Exemplary Chutzpah, QC).

Edmund Burke had a word for it:

I saw her just above the horizon, decorating and cheering the elevated sphere she just began to move in, glittering like the morning star, full of life, and splendour, and joy. Little did I dream that I should have lived to see disasters fallen upon her in a nation of gallant men, in a nation of men of honour, and of cavaliers. I thought ten thousand swords must have leaped from their scabbards to avenge even a look that threatened her with insult. But the age of chivalry is gone.

It is indeed; now it is buttocks that leap, not swords, and trousers, not scabbards, that they leap from. And the men's action is no less disgraceful merely

168

because they were apparently under the impression that Lady Caroline was there to demonstrate against nuclear missiles, for apart from anything else, if they will show their buttocks to a lady of title what might they not reveal to the more humbly born? As Lady Caroline said, 'I sympathise with any woman who has to put up with anything like this, regardless of her political allegiance.' And to make matters still worse – if anything *could* be worse than what I have described – the Thames Valley police, when questioned about the matter, said that they knew nothing about it, and added that 'the whole affair should be taken with a pinch of salt.'

At this point, as those who know me will readily suppose, I sent for my horsewhip and looked up the trains to Greenham. What? Insult a nobleman's sister, scion of a marquessate whose origins are lost in the mists of unimaginable antiquity (it goes back to 1888), a shy and tender maiden cloistered until now amid the echoing halls of

Clandeboye, the even tenor of her days disturbed by nothing more sensational than a discussion of farm prices over afternoon tea with the McGillicuddy of the Reeks? Do this, and hope to escape a thrashing at the hands of the Chevalier Levin? Perish the thought!

But while I was waiting for the taxi to take me to the station, I read on, and the subtle worm of doubt began to gnaw at the foundations of my anger. In the first place, Lady Caroline added one piece of information that would surely have been better left unadded: 'I don't know if they were Americans', she said, 'because I only saw their buttocks.' (If they had been Russians, of course, they would have had snow on their bottoms.) But it was what followed that caused me to wonder just what I would be getting into if I took action to avenge this stain upon a lady's honour.

For it seems that Lady Caroline, so far from being, as I had assumed, a chit of seventeen who would blush scarlet at the name of Edgar Allan Poe, is a fifty-one-year-old novelist (she writes as Caroline Blackwood) who has been married no fewer than three times, and more to the point (in view of her unwillingness to assign a nationality to the offending buttocks), two of her husbands were American and one British. Not to put too fine a point on it, Lady Caroline has been around.

Her first troth (Marr. diss.) was plighted to Mr Lucian Freud, the painter. Her second hubby (Marr. diss.) was Israel Citkowitz, an American composer. *En troisièmes noces,* she was spliced to Robert Lowell, the poet, who left her a widow in 1977. Now it is no doubt possible that each of these distinguished men invariably wore long woollen combinations while taking a bath, and came to bed clad in a suit of armour. But the hypothesis is sufficiently improbable to be ignored. To speak plainly, I think she has seen a male buttock to two in her time, up to a maximum of six (reckoning two to a husband).

True, a matrimonial buttock bared in the course of domesticity is a far cry from a busload of strangers' buttocks bared to make a political comment; moreover, and irrespective of the intention behind the Greenham buttocks, one can have too much even of a good thing – a chocolate with my coffee is always welcome, but a couple of dozen would tend to cloy, and it may be that what bittermints are to me buttocks are to Lady Caroline. All the same, I have a horrible feeling that I am about to recite the whole of a limerick that begins 'There was a young man of Australia, Who painted his bum as a dahlia. . .' (What is more, in view of the somewhat anatomical paintings of ladies in her first husband's *oeuvre*, she is lucky not to find a more than lifesize portrait of her *pudendum* hanging in the Tate.)

You see, I am sure, what I am driving at. If not, I can make it clear by asking a question. Lady Caroline says that she was 'shocked and appalled.' And my question is. *Was* she? I mean *really?* Really and actually shocked and appalled?

Honest? See this wet, see this dry, cross my heart and hope to die? Not just shocked or just appalled but *both?* Furthermore, Lady Caroline says she has 'never seen something so unpleasant.' Never? *Never?* After all, we have established with reasonable certainty that she must have known what a buttock looks like. We also know, because she tells us as much, that she 'only saw their buttocks', which rules out the possibility that in the course of the proceedings the offending airmen-turned round. (Mind you, even if they had ...). Yet she has never seen something so unpleasant.

Au font, if I may so express myself, it all comes back to my grandmother's celebrated dictum: if you never have anything worse than that to worry about, you won't have done too badly. If Lady Caroline never has greater reason to be shocked and appalled, if she never sees something more unpleasant, than the sight of a row of men's buttocks, she can count herself lucky indeed. The world is full of wars and the rumours of wars;

famine, pestilence and sudden death are not yet eradicated, the heart of man still contains ample store of envy, hatred, malice and all uncharitableness. Here, milady, is a leper; over there, an orphaned child weeps; anon comes a procession of beggars, their tin cups empty as their stomachs; that thwack you hear is a tyrant's truncheon on an innocent head.

Still shocked, still appalled, still never seen something so unpleasant? Go to, you great ninny; next time a platoon of airmen, or for that matter an entire regiment of soldiers, show their bottoms to you, try laughing, and if you cannot laugh, turn your head away, and be about your business. Otherwise, I warn you, I shall tell yet again, with a wealth of expression and many a meaningful glance, the story of the old woman who calls a policeman to her home and bids him arrest the man in the house opposite for gross indecency, explaining that the neighbour in question is standing stark naked in a brightly lit and uncurtained window. The policeman peers out, but says he can see no such sight. 'Of course not', snaps the crone, 'you have to stand on a chair.'

The Times March 24, 1984

Living by his wits

A Cup of News: The Life of Thomas Nashe
by Charles Nicholl*

Every age has its literary under-
world, just round the corner from
Grub Street, where live those truly
talented writers who cannot find (or keep)
a patron, who drank the advance and sell
an entirely different book to an entirely
different publisher, who find quarrel in a
straw and usually choose those who can
harm them to quarrel with. Some of them
will turn their hands to anything that can
be done with a pen, not excluding
pornography, begging letters, forgery,

*Routledge & Kegan Paul, 1984.

plagiarism and blackmail. Mock them not; they include Chatterton, Corvo, Aretino, Villon himself.

And Thomas Nashe, of whom we have here at last a substantial and scholarly biography. The Elizabethan literary swamp was the most fetid of all; in it there splashed strange beasts – poets and playwrights and pamphleteers who doubled as spies for the Government or the Government's enemies, men who would one day join a plot against the Queen and the next day betray it, secret Papists and noisy Puritans, alchemists and necromancers, Raleigh factions and Leicester factions.

In this seething stew of literature, politics, diabolism, printing and religion bobbed Nashe, who has the honour of being the author of the very first printed reference to Shakespeare. He was one of the 'University Wits'; he lived not more than thirty-four years; he wrote plays (one of them, a joint work with Ben Jonson, was suppressed as slanderous and seditious, and Nashe had to go into hiding while Jonson went to gaol), pamphlets, invective, polemic, the earliest narrative poem about a dildo, the first picaresque novel. He was almost always broke and frequently drunk; he had a giant fit of remorse in mid-career, and wrote a half-mad religious tract in consequence; his last, strangest and finest work was a disquisition in praise of the red herring, a most fitting apotheosis.

Nashe is best known for his part in the 'Martin Marprelate' controversy. This was the pseudonym of a shifting collective of Puritans, publishing their tracts in *samizdat;* their chief target was episcopacy. For Martin, an Anglican Bishop was little better than the Pope; Whitgift, the Archbishop of Cantebury, was 'John of Cant' and 'the pope of Lambehithe.' Whitgift had the idea of casting out Satan with Beelzebub; he enlisted Nashe, among others, to write counter-Martinist tracts and pamphlets, using all Martin's own devices of wit, satire and scurrility.

Such work was right up Nashe's alley,

and he did it with such gusto that he frightened his patron into suppressing his later offerings, a perfect instance of Nashe's damaging his prospects by his inability to let well alone. Mr Nicholl suggests that Nashe was a secret Catholic sympathiser, and offers some suggestive titbits to back up his claim. Unfortunately, he then rapidly succumbs to an almost fatal attack of the Spotted Hotsons, in which delirium he can and does make any phrase, however innocuous, pregnant with hidden meanings and allusions ('Once the signal is noticed the whole concealed message becomes clear'); when the fit is most strongly upon him, his 'discoveries' are hardly to be distinguished from the ravings of the Baconians (he even offers a ludicrously feeble cypher for the identification of Holofernes with Florio).

Most scholars agree that Nashe is portrayed by Shakespeare as Moth in *Love's Labour's Lost,* and Mr Nicholl does not dissent from the prevailing view, though I must say I am tempted to see him in Yorick, for he was certainly capable of pouring a flagon of Rhenish on anybody's head. But what has been hitherto neglected, and even by Mr Nicholl is not treated as fully as it might be, is Nashe's extraordinary use of language, which brings to mind Rabelais and Rabelais's translator Urquhart, together with some of the most extreme apocalyptic writing of the two and seventy jarring sects which sprang up in the wake of the Civil War, and indeed even some modern surrealists. Here, for instance, are some of the names he invented to abuse his great enemy, Gabriel Harvey: Gaffer Jobbernoule, Gamaliel Hobgoblin, Gilgilis Hobberdehoy, Gregory Habberdine, Gabriel Hangtelow, Timothy Tiptoes, Braggadochio Glorioso, Infractissime Pistlepragmos, Gibralter, Galpogas and Gabrielissime. And here – it has to be quoted at length if it is to have its effect – is Nashe's terrible and terrified vision of the evil that boiled about him:

What do we talke of one divel? There

is not a room in anie mans house but is pestred and close packed with a campe royall of divels . . . No place (bee it no bigger than a pockhole in a mans face) but is close thronged with them. Infinite millions of them wil hang swarming about a worm-eaten nose. Don Lucifer himselfe, their grand Capitano, asketh no better throne than a bleare eye to set up his state in. Upon a haire they will sit like a nit, and over-dredge a bald pate like a white scurffe . . . . In Westminster Hall a man can scarce breath for them, for in every corner they hover as thick as moates in the sunne. The Druides that dwelt in the Isle of Man, which are famous for great conjurers, are reported to have been louise with familiars. Had they but put their finger and their thumbe into their neck, they could have pluckt out a whole neast of them.

The obvious question is: is there really enough of Nashe for him to deserve a biography of his own rather than a chapter in someone else's? It is true that Mr Nicholl is sometimes hard pressed. He offers, for instance, fourteen pages of close textual and thematic analysis of a play, *The Isle of Dogs,* of which not a single line apart from the title has survived in print or manuscript, and of which nothing at all is known; a considerable achievement. But there is remarkably little padding elsewhere, nor much need of it; Nashe comes alive in Mr Nicholl's hands, and in doing so demands to be taken seriously; even the author's penchant for seeing things that are not there does not get in the way. Nashe did have genius, warped though it was, and his best work will survive, undamaged by his scribbled worst. And he made friends; he even kept some, one of whom wrote a fitting epitaph:

His stile was wittie, though it had
    some gall,
Some thing he might have mended,
    so may all.

Yet this I say, that for a mother witt,
Fewe men have ever seene the like
  of it.
                    Observer March 25th, 1984

Sinister rituals

What would you think if you learnt that the Labour group on Lewisham council had formally declared that membership of the Labour Party was incompatible with being a Jew, and that they were now considering an extension of this doctrine, to the effect that no Jew could be a member of the council staff, so that it would follow from such a rule (for Lewisham council is Labour-controlled) that Jewish employees would be dismissed? Before you consider that question, add this one to it (they can probably be answered together): how would you feel if you were told on good authority that in Islington, applicants for jobs on the council's staff are to be required to reveal whether they are Jews?

Hang on a minute: I want to extend the questionnaire. Suppose you picked up the *Guardian* and in it read an item which consisted of nothing but a list of prominent British citizens who, the writer was claiming to reveal, were Jews, with the implication that they concealed the fact: what would your attitude be to that? And what would it be if you read such an item in that newspaper on several days in succession, with a fresh register each day of undercover Jews?

I could go on like this for some time. Well, I *will*. Describe your feelings on learning that someone had written a book demonstrating (to the author's satisfaction at least) that the Jack the Ripper murders had been committed by a group of men directed by a Jew, the purpose being to hush up a royal scandal which the victims had learnt about, that the mutilations to the women's bodies were in the form of the Jewish Star of

David, and that there had been Jewish conspiracy at the highest level to conceal the Jewish guilt for the crimes. Then, if you will be so kind, consider carefully what would be the nature of your response if you read a more recent book by the same author, sub-titled *The Secret World of the Jews,* in which the writer reveals that he had written to the Lord Chief Justice, the Master of the Rolls, the President of the Family Division of the High Court and the Vice-Chancellor of the Chancery Division of the same, demanding to know whether they were or were not Jews, and clearly felt it very significant, even sinister, that three of them threw his letter into the wastepaper basket and that the reply of the fourth was 'I do not really feel that quesiton of whether or not I am a Jew is a matter of public concern.'

And finally, just before I reveal what all this is about, tell me what you would think if you read through the whole of the 'Are you a Jew, judge?' book and found it to be composed largely of anonymous tittle-tattle about the hidden but enormous and widespread influence of the Jews in British life eked out by a substantial amount of the kind of stuff otherwise found only in the letters of those who write to me in green ink to reveal that the Archbishop of Canterbury is putting thought-rays into their heads from outer space, and to insist that I should stop him forthwith.

Very well, then; get another cup of coffee and make yourself comfortable. Then, with a red pencil for ease of reference, strike through every mention of Jews in what you have just read, and substitute, as the sense requires, 'Mason', 'Masons', 'Masonic', etc. And *now* tell me what you feel when I say that, when thus – and only thus – amended, every single word I have written is the literal truth. In Lewisham and Islington such steps *have* been taken against Masons; such daily lists of alleged Masons *did* appear in the *Guardian;* there *is* such a book about the Masonic nature of Jack the Ripper's crimes, Masonic mutilations and all (the book is sub-titled, with almost unbelievable insensitivity, *The Final Solution*); the same author, Mr Stephen Knight, *has* just written such a successor, called in full *The Brotherhood: The Secret World of the Freemasons*, in which he reveals that he *did* write to the four senior judges of England, demanding to be told whether they were Masons, and does make clear that he thinks their failure to comply a matter for suspicion.

As David Hume would point out even if I do not, it does not logically follow that because one group of people are innocent of the vile charges brought collectively against them another must be equally blameless; I cannot prove tht there is no sinister international body working to take over the world with the aid of a plan called *The Protocols of the Elders of Freemasonry.* But it is worth remarking that the nature of many of the charges against Freemasons is astonishingly similar to that of many accusations made against Jews by anti-semites, and that the most virulent of Jew-baiters have commonly been Mason-haters as well. And anyway, what is the difference between a threat to sack Masons just because they are Masons and a threat to sack Jews just because they are Jews?

The point about charges of collective guilt is that they can never be disproved; if a particular Freemason can show beyond any doubt that he has never exerted, or been the beneficiary of, improper Masonic influence or behaviour, the reply of the people like Mr Stephen Knight will always be: of course not, it's the other Masons I am talking about. And since there must be bad men who are Masons, as there are bad men who are Jews, and some Masons who help fellow-Masons to preferment or gain, as there are some Jews who do such things for fellow-Jews (and some supporters of Tottenham Hotspur for *their* chums, and some cat-lovers likewise, and some farmers, and some Rastafarians, and some Roman Catholics – ooh, I could tell you a thing or two about what Roman Catholics get up to with their sinister rituals like 'Communion' and 'Confession' and 'Mass' – and some Glaswegians, and some nuclear disarmers, and for that matter some writers of rubbishy books), it will always be possible, on the principle of *crimine ab uno, disce omnes,* to make a number of individuals who have one, and only one, thing in common look like a single many-headed entity whose common element, because it is wrongly used by some of them, is itself and of its very nature to be condemned.

When this practice is directed against Jews, it is called anti-semitism. When it is directed against black people, it is called racism. When it is directed against the uneducated, it is called class prejudice. When it is directed against strange old women, it is called witch-hunting. But when it is directed against Freemasons, it is apparently all quite right and proper, at any rate in the eyes of those responsible for the diary of the *Guardian,* in the eyes of those who write books to show that the Jack the Ripper murders were the product of a Masonic conspiracy and follow these up with books which suggest that practically *everything* is the product of a Masonic conspiracy, and in the eyes of those who control the councils of Lewisham and Islington together with, if this evil thing is not crushed now, many another council up and down the land.

I do not suppose that Mr Knight's books and the *Guardian* diary are written with intent to cause harm; nor would I be in favour of censorship of them even if I did. But they are harbingers of a foul spring. And when it comes to the interrogation in Lewisham and Islington of council members and employees as to their Masonic affiliations, no doubt conducted by specially appointed Mason-sniffers like the Jew-sniffers of yesteryear, followed by threats of expulsion or dismissal for those who give off the telltale sulphurous stink, then – why then, I think, it is time for us to take down from the wall the weapons which we fondly believed could be left to gather rust forever, and lay about us with a will, going into battle beneath a banner embroidered with Santayana's words: Those who cannot remember the past are condemned to repeat it.

The Times March 27th, 1984

The aim of Masterworks Large Print Books is to make reading a more rewarding experience for partially sighted people.

A good range of recreational reading is available in large print, but there remains a shortage of fine literature, and it is the intention of Masterworks to make good this deficiency, by publishing large print editions of erudite titles. Wherever practible, works by winners of the Nobel Prize for Literature will be chosen, together with titles by other distinguished writers.

Type sizes and faces have been carefully researched, and the contrast between the black type and the cream tint of the lightweight paper has been calculated to cause a minimum of strain to the eyes.

All the texts have been completely reset, because of the importance of good type design in books catering for partially sighted readers. The results of research suggest that four different factors are critical in the typography of large print books: the size of the type, its boldness, the way it is spaced, and the use of a consistent typeface. A proper combination of the best typographic features results in a vast improvement in readability.

We would like as many people as possible to be aware of these innovations in large print and hope that readers will recommend the results to others. We welcome suggestions from readers for new titles.

Other titles in this series:

Virginia Woolf

FLUSH

This reconstruction of the life of Flush, Elizabeth Barrett Browning's spaniel, throws an intimate light on the famous romance – unachievable by any other means.

'Her passionate love, not only for the big moments of life, but also for its daily humdrum details will remain an example that is at once an inspiration and a judge.'
W H Auden on Virginia Woolf.

Heinrich Böll

THE LOST HONOUR OF KATHARINA BLUM

Pretty, bright young Katharina Blum falls in love with a young radical lawbreaker on the run from the police. Portrayed by the local press as a whore, a communist sympathizer and an atheist, she becomes the target of anonymous phone calls and threats. Her life ruined and her character and honour trampled by the distortions of a corrupt press she shoots the offending journalist.

This novel is a masterful comment on the law and the press, the labyrinth of social truth, and the relentless collision of fact and fiction.

Margaret Yourcenar
ORIENTAL TALES

Translated from the French by Alberto Manguel in collaboration with the author.

From China to Greece, from the Balkans to Japan, these tales take us from a portrait of the painter Wang-Fo, 'who loves the image of things and not the things themselves' and whose own work saves him from execution, to legends of a hero betrayed and then rescued by love, and to the Indian goddess Kali, who in her unhappiness discovers 'the emptiness of desire'. Violence, murder and betrayal all feature in these stories of love and adventure.

Edmund Wilson

MEMOIRS OF HECATE COUNTY

The mud of Hecate County is steamy, infested with snapping turtles, the suburban streets contrast with the once-white balconies and lush vegetation of the decaying mansions – both harbour wasted talents, lingering resentments and heady passions. The young narrator enters into every part of life there, seduced by the charm and corruption in the atmosphere as much as by the ghostly Ellen Terhune or the erotic possibilities of the Princess with the Golden Hair.